The Great Conspiracy - Part VII

JOHN ALEXANDER LOGAN

New York 1886

TABLE OF CONTENTS

FREEDOM AT LAST ASSURED

As to the Military situation, a few words are, at this time, necessary: Hood had now marched Northward, with some 50,000 men, toward Nashville, Tenn., while Sherman, leaving Thomas and some 35,000 men behind, to thwart him, had abandoned his base, and was marching Southward from Atlanta, through Georgia, toward the Sea.

On the 30th of November, 1864, General Schofield, in command of the 4th and 23rd Corps of Thomas's Army, decided to make a stand against Hood's Army, at Franklin, in the angle of the Harpeth river, in order to give time for the Union supply-trains to cross the river. Here, with less than 20,000 Union troops, behind some hastily constructed works, he had received the impetuous and overwhelming assault of the Enemy—at first so successful as to threaten a bloody and disastrous rout to the Union troops—and, by a brilliant counter-charge, and subsequent obstinate defensive-fighting, had repulsed the Rebel forces, with nearly three times the Union losses, and withdrew the next day in safety to the defenses of Nashville.

A few days later, Hood, with his diminished Rebel Army, sat down before the lines of Thomas's somewhat augmented Army, which stretched from bank to bank of the bight of the Cumberland river upon which Nashville is situated.

And now a season of intense cold set in, lasting a week or ten days. During this period of apparent inaction on both sides—which aroused public apprehension in the North, and greatly disturbed General Grant—I was ordered to City Point, by the General-in-Chief, with a view to his detailing me to Thomas's Command, at Nashville.

On the way, I called on President Lincoln, at the White House. I found him not very well, and with his feet considerably swollen. He was sitting on a chair, with his feet resting on a table, while a barber was shaving him. Shaking him by the hand, and asking after his health, he answered, with a humorous twinkle of the eye, that he would illustrate his condition by telling me a story. Said he: "Two of my neighbors, on a certain occasion, swapped horses. One of these horses was large, but quite thin. A few days after, on inquiry being made of the man who had the big boney horse, how the animal was getting along?—whether improving or not?—the owner said he was doing finely; that he had fattened almost up to the knees already!"

Afterward—when, the process of shaving had been completed, we passed to another room—our conversation naturally turned upon the War; and his ideas upon all subjects connected with it were as clear as those of any other person with whom I ever talked. He had an absolute conviction as to the ultimate outcome of the War—the final triumph of the Union Arms; and I well remember, with what an air of complete relief and perfect satisfaction he said to me, referring to Grant—"We have now at the head of the Armies, a man in whom all the People can have confidence."

But to return to Military operations: On December 10th? Sherman reached the sea-board and commenced the siege of Savannah, Georgia; on the 13th, Fort McAllister was stormed and Sherman's communications opened with the Sea; on the 15th and 16th, the great Battle of Nashville was fought, between the Armies of Thomas and Hood, and a glorious victory gained by the Union Arms—Hood's Rebel forces being routed, pursued for days, and practically dispersed; and, before the year ended, Savannah surrendered, and was presented to the Nation, as "a Christmas gift," by Sherman.

And now the last Session of the Thirty-eighth Congress having commenced, the Thirteenth Amendment might at any time come up again in the House. In his fourth and last Annual Message, just sent in to that Body, President Lincoln had said:

"At the last Session of Congress a proposed Amendment of the Constitution abolishing Slavery throughout the United States, passed the Senate, but failed for lack of the requisite two-thirds vote in the House of Representatives. Although the present is the same Congress, and nearly the same members, and without questioning the wisdom or patriotism of those who stood in opposition, I venture to recommend the reconsideration and passage of the measure at the present Session. Of course the abstract question is not changed; but an intervening election shows, almost certainly, that the next Congress will pass the measure if this does not. Hence there is only a question of time as to when the proposed Amendment will go to, the States for their action. And as it is to so go, at all, events, may we not agree that the sooner the better? It is not claimed that the election has imposed a duty on members to change their views or their votes, any farther than, as an additional element to be considered, their judgment may be affected by it. It is the voice of the People now, for the first time, heard upon the question. In a great National crisis like ours, unanimity of action among those seeking a common end is very desirable—almost indispensable. And yet no approach to such unanimity is attainable unless some deference shall be paid to the will of the majority simply because it is the will of the majority. In this case the common end is the maintenance of the Union; and, among the means to secure that end, such will, through the election, is most clearly declared in favor of such Constitutional Amendment."

After affirming that, on the subject of the preservation of the Union, the recent elections had shown the existence of "no diversity among the People;" that "we have more men now than we had when the War began;" that "we are gaining strength" in all ways; and that, after the evidences given by Jefferson Davis of his unchangeable opposition to accept anything short of severance from the Union, "no attempt at negotiation with the Insurgent leader could result in any good," he appealed to the other Insurgents to come back to the fold—the door of amnesty and pardon, being still "open to all." But, he continued:

"In presenting the abandonment of armed resistance to the National Authority, on the part of the Insurgents, as the only indispensable condition to ending the War, on the part of the Government, I retract nothing heretofore said as to Slavery. I repeat the declaration made a year ago, that 'while I remain in my present position I shall not attempt to retract or modify the Emancipation Proclamation, nor shall I return to Slavery any Person who is Free by the terms of that Proclamation, or by any of the Acts of Congress.' If the People should, by whatever mode or means, make it an Executive duty to Reenslave such Persons, another, and not I, must be their instrument to perform it. In stating a single condition of Peace I mean simply to say that the War will cease on the part of the Government, whenever it shall have ceased on the part of those who began it."

On the 22d of December, 1864, in accordance with the terms of a Concurrent Resolution that had passed both Houses, Congress adjourned until January 5, 1865. During the Congressional Recess, however, Mr. Lincoln, anxious for the fate of the Thirteenth Amendment, exerted himself, as it afterward appeared, to some purpose, in its behalf, by inviting private conferences with him, at the White House, of such of the Border-State and other War-Democratic Representatives as had before voted against the measure, but whose general character gave him ground for hoping that they might not be altogether deaf to the voice of reason and patriotism.

[Among those for whom he sent was Mr. Rollins, of Missouri, who afterward gave the following interesting account of the interview:

"The President had several times in my presence expressed his deep anxiety in favor of the passage of this great measure. He and others had repeatedly counted votes in order to ascertain, as far as they could, the strength of the measure upon a second trial in the House. He was doubtful about its passage, and some ten days or two weeks before it came up for consideration in the House, I received a note from him, written in pencil on a card, while sitting at my desk in the House, stating that he wished to see me, and asking that I call on him at the White House. I responded that I would be there the next morning at nine o'clock.

"I was prompt in calling upon him and found him alone in his office. He received me in the most cordial manner, and said in his usual familiar way: 'Rollins, I have been wanting to talk to you for some time about the Thirteenth Amendment proposed to the Constitution of the United States, which will have to be voted on now, before a great while.'

"I said: 'Well, I am here, and ready to talk upon that subject.

"He said: 'You and I were old Whigs, both of us followers of that great statesman, Henry Clay, and I tell you I never had an opinion upon the subject of Slavery in my life that I did not get from him. I am very anxious that the War should be brought to a close at the earliest possible date, and I don't believe this can be accomplished as long as those fellows down South can rely upon the Border-States to help them; but if the Members from the Border-States would unite, at least enough of them to pass the Thirteenth Amendment to the Constitution, they would soon see that they could not expect much help from that quarter, and be willing to give up their opposition and quit their War upon the Government; that is my chief hope and main reliance to bring the War to a speedy close, and I have sent for you as an old Whig friend to come and see me, that I might make an appeal to you to vote for this Amendment. It is going to be very close; a few votes one way or the other will decide it.'

"To this, I responded: 'Mr. President, so far as I am concerned, you need not have sent for me to ascertain my views on this subject, for although I represent perhaps the strongest Slave-district in Missouri, and have the misfortune to be one of the largest Slave-owners in the country where I reside, I had already determined to vote for the Amendment.

"He arose from his chair, and grasping me by the hand, gave it a hearty shake, and said: 'I am most delighted to hear that.'

"He asked me how many more of the Missouri delegates in the House would vote for it.

"I said I could not tell; the Republicans of course would; General Loan, Mr. Blow, Mr. Boyd, and Colonel McClurg.

"He said, 'Won't General Price vote for it? He is a good Union man.' I said I could not answer.

"'Well, what about General King?'

"I told him I did not know.

"He then asked about Judges Hall and Norton.

"I said they would both vote against it, I thought.

"'Well,' he said, 'are you on good terms with Price and King?'

"I responded in the affirmative, and that I was on easy terms with the entire delegation.

"He then asked me if I would not talk with those who might be persuaded to vote for the amendment, and report to him as soon as I could find out what the prospect was.'

"I answered that I would do so with pleasure, and remarked at the same time, that when I was a young man, in 1848, I was the Whig competitor of King for Governor of Missouri, and, as he beat me very badly, I thought now he should pay me back by voting as I desired him on this important question.

"I promised the President I would talk to this gentleman upon the subject.

"He said: 'I would like you to talk to all the Border-State men whom you can approach properly, and tell them of my anxiety to have the measure pass; and let me know the prospect of the Border-State vote,' which I promised to do.

"He again said: 'The passage of this Amendment will clinch the whole subject; it will bring the War, I have no doubt, rapidly to a close.'"—Arnold's Life of Lincoln, pp. 358-359,]

On the 5th of January, 1865, the Christmas Recess having expired, Congress re-assembled. The motion to reconsider the vote-by which the Joint Resolution, to amend the Constitution by the abolition of Slavery, had been defeated—was not called up, on that day, as its friends had not all returned; but the time was mainly consumed in able speeches, by Mr. Creswell of Maryland, and Stevens of Pennsylvania, in which the former declared that "whether we would or not, we must establish Freedom if we would exterminate Treason. Events have left us no choice. The People have learned their duty and have instructed us accordingly." And Mr. Thaddeus Stevens solemnly said: "We are about to ascertain the National will, by another vote to amend the Constitution. If gentlemen opposite will yield to the voice of God and Humanity, and vote for it, I verily believe the sword of the Destroying Angel will be stayed, and this People be reunited. If we still harden our hearts, and blood must still flow, may the ghosts of the slaughtered victims sit heavily upon the souls of those who cause it!"

On the 6th of January, Mr. Ashley called up his motion to reconsider the vote defeating the Thirteenth Amendment, and opened the debate with a lengthy and able speech in favor of that measure, in concluding which he said:

"The genius of history, with iron pen, is waiting to record our verdict where it will remain forever for all the coming generations of men to approve or condemn. God grant that this verdict may be one over which the friends of Liberty, impartial and universal, in this Country and Europe, and in every

Land beneath the sun, may rejoice; a verdict which shall declare that America is Free; a verdict which shall add another day of jubilee, and the brightest of all, to our National calendar."

The debate was participated in by nearly all the prominent men, on both sides of the House—the speeches of Messrs. Cox, Brooks, Voorhees, Mallory, Holman, Woods and Pendleton being the most notable, in opposition to, and those of Scofield, Rollins, Garfield and Stevens, in favor of, the Amendment. That of Scofield probably stirred up "the adversary" more thoroughly than any other; that of Rollins was more calculated to conciliate and capture the votes of hesitating, or Border-State men; that of Garfield was perhaps the most scholarly and eloquent; while that of Stevens was remarkable for its sledge-hammer pungency and characteristic brevity.

Mr. Pendleton, toward the end of his speech, had said of Mr. Stevens: "Let him be careful, lest when the passions of these times be passed away, and the historian shall go back to discover where was the original infraction of the Constitution, he may find that sin lies at the door of others than the people now in arms." And it was this that brought the sterling old Patriot again to his feet, in vindication of the acts of his liberty-inspired life, and in defense of the power to amend the Constitution, which had been assailed.

The personal antithesis with which he concluded his remarks was in itself most dramatically effective, Said he:

"So far as the appeals of the learned gentleman (Mr. Pendleton) are concerned, in his pathetic winding up, I will be willing to take my chance, when we all moulder in the dust. He may have his epitaph written, if it be truly written, 'Here rests the ablest and most pertinacious defender of Slavery, and opponent of Liberty;' and I will be satisfied if my epitaph shall be written thus: 'Here lies one who never rose to any eminence, and who only courted the low ambition to have it said that he had striven to ameliorate the condition of the poor, the lowly, the downtrodden, of every race, and language, and color.'"

As he said these words, the crowded floors and galleries broke out into involuntary applause for the grand "Old Commoner"—who only awaited its cessation, to caustically add: "I shall be content, with such a eulogy on his lofty tomb and such an inscription on my humble grave, to trust our memories to the judgment of after ages."

The debate, frequently interrupted by Appropriation Bills, and other important and importunate measures, lasted until the 31st of January, when Mr. Ashley called the previous question on his motion to reconsider.

Mr. Stiles at once moved to table the motion to reconsider. Mr. Stiles's motion was lost by 57 yeas to 111 nays. This was in the nature of a test-vote, and the result, when announced, was listened to, with breathless attention, by the crowded House and galleries. It was too close for either side to be satisfied; but it showed a gain to the friends of the Amendment;

that was something. How the final vote would be, none could tell. Meanwhile it was known, from the announcements on the floor, that Rogers was absent through his own illness and Voorhees through illness in his family.

The previous question being seconded and the main question ordered, the yeas and nays were called on the motion to reconsider—and the intense silence succeeding the monotonous calling of the names was broken by the voice of the Speaker declaring the motion to reconsider, carried, by 112 yeas to 57 nays.

This vote created a slight sensation. There was a gain of one, (English), at any rate, from among those not voting on the previous motion. Now, if there should be but the change of a single vote, from the nays to the yeas, the Amendment would be carried!

The most intensely anxious solicitude was on nearly every face, as Mr. Mallory, at this critical moment, made the point of order that "a vote to reconsider the vote by which the subject now before the House was disposed of, in June last, requires two-thirds of this Body," and emphatically added: "that two-thirds vote has not been obtained."

A sigh of relief swept across the galleries, as the Speaker overruled the point of order. Other attempted interruptions being resolutely met and defeated by Mr. Ashley, in charge of the Resolution, the "previous question" was demanded, seconded, and the main question ordered—which was on the passage of the Resolution.

And now, amid the hush of a breathless and intent anxiety—so absolute that the scratch of the recording pencil could be heard—the Clerk commenced to call the roll!

So consuming was the solicitude, on all sides, for the fate of this portentous measure, that fully one-half the Representatives kept tally at their desks as the vote proceeded, while the heads of the gathered thousands of both sexes, in the galleries, craned forward, as though fearing to lose the startlingly clear responses, while the roll-call progressed.

When it reached the name of English—Governor English, a Connecticut Democrat, who had not voted on the first motion, to table the motion to reconsider, but had voted "yea" on the motion to reconsider,—and he responded with a clear-cut "aye" on the passage of the Resolution—it looked as though light were coming at last, and applause involuntarily broke forth from the Republican side of the floor, spreading instantly to the galleries, despite the efforts of the Speaker to preserve order.

So, when Ganson of New York, and other Democrats, voted "aye," the applause was renewed again and again, and still louder again, when, with smiling face—which corroborated the thrilling, fast-spreading, whisper, that "the Amendment is safe!"—Speaker Colfax directed the Clerk to call his name, as a member of the House, and, in response to that call, voted "aye!"

Then came dead silence, as the Clerk passed the result to the Speaker—during which a pin might have been heard to drop,—broken at last by the Speaker's ringing voice: "The Constitutional majority of two-thirds having voted in the affirmative, the Joint Resolution is passed."

[The enrolled Resolution received the approval and signature of the President, Feb. 1, 1865,]

The words had scarcely left the Speaker's lips, when House and galleries sprang to their feet, clapping their hands, stamping their feet, waving hats and handkerchiefs, and cheering so loudly and so long that it seemed as if this great outburst of enthusiasm—indulged in, in defiance of all parliamentary rules—would never cease!

In his efforts to control it, Speaker Colfax hammered the desk until he nearly broke his mallet. Finally, by 4 o'clock, P.M., after several minutes of useless effort—during which the pounding of the mallet was utterly lost in the noisy enthusiasm and excitement, in which both the Freedom-loving men and women of the Land, there present, participated—the Speaker at last succeeded in securing a lull.

Advantage was instantly taken of it, by the successor of the dead Owen Lovejoy, Mr. Ingersoll of Illinois, his young face flushing with the glow of patriotism, as he cried: "Mr. Speaker! In honor of this Immortal and Sublime Event I move that the House do now adjourn." The Speaker declared the motion carried, amid renewed demonstrations of enthusiasm.

During all these uncontrollable ebullitions of popular feeling in behalf of personal Liberty and National Freedom and strength, the Democratic members of the House had sat, many of them moving uneasily in their seats, with chagrin painted in deep lines upon their faces, while others were bolt upright, as if riveted to their chairs, looking straight before them at the Speaker, in a vain attempt, belied by the pallid anger of their set countenances, to appear unconscious of the storm of popular feeling breaking around them, which they now doggedly perceived might be but a forecast of the joyful enthusiasm which on that day, and on the morrow, would spread from one end of the Land to the other.

Harris, of Maryland, made a sort of "Last Ditch" protest against adjournment, by demanding the "yeas and nays" on the motion to adjourn. The motion was, however, carried, by 121 yeas to 24 nays; and, as the members left their places in the Hall—many of them to hurry with their hearty congratulations to President Lincoln at the White House—the triumph, in the Halls of our National Congress, of Freedom and Justice and Civilization, over Slavery and Tyranny and Barbarism, was already being saluted by the booming of one hundred guns on Capitol Hill.

How large a share was Mr. Lincoln's, in that triumph, these pages have already sufficiently indicated. Sweet indeed must have been the joy that thrilled his whole being, when, sitting in the White House, he heard the bellowing artillery attest the success of his labors in behalf of Emancipation. Proud indeed must he have felt when, the following night, in response to the loud and jubilant cries of "Lincoln!" "Lincoln!" "Abe Lincoln!" "Uncle Abe!" and other affectionate calls, from a great concourse of people who, with music, had assembled outside the White House to give him a grand serenade and popular ovation, he appeared at an open window, bowed to the tumult of their acclamations, and declared that "The great Job is ended!"—adding, among other things, that the occasion was one fit for congratulation, and, said he, "I cannot but congratulate all present—myself, the Country, and the whole World—upon this great moral victory. * * * This ends the Job!"

Substantially the job was ended. There was little doubt, after such a send off, by the President and by Congress, in view of the character of the State Legislatures, as well as the temper of the People, that the requisite number of States would be secured to ratify the Thirteenth Amendment. Already, on the 1st of February, that is to say, on the very day of this popular demonstration at the Executive Mansion, the President's own State, Illinois, had ratified it—and this circumstance added to the satisfaction and happiness which beamed from, and almost made beautiful, his homely face. Other States quickly followed; Maryland, on February 1st and 3rd; Rhode Island and Michigan, on February 2nd; New York, February 2nd and 3rd; West Virginia, February 3rd; Maine and Kansas, February 7th; Massachusetts and Pennsylvania, February 8th; Virginia, February 9th; Ohio and Missouri, February 10th; Nevada and Indiana, February 16th; Louisiana, February 17th; Minnesota, February 8th and 23rd; Wisconsin, March 1st; Vermont, March 9th; Tennessee, April 5th and 7th; Arkansas, April 20th; Connecticut, May 5th; New Hampshire, July 1st; South Carolina, November 13th; Alabama, December 2nd; North Carolina, December 4th; Georgia, December 9th; Oregon, December 11th; California, December 20th; and Florida, December 28th;—all in 1865; with New Jersey, closely following, on January 23rd; and Iowa, January 24th;—in 1866.

Long ere this last date, however, the Secretary of State (Mr. Seward) had been able to, and did, announce (November 18, 1865) the ratification of the Amendment by the requisite number of States, and certified that the same had "become, to all intents and purposes, valid as a part of the Constitution of the United States."

Not until then, was "the job" absolutely ended; but, as has been already mentioned, it was, at the time Mr. Lincoln spoke, as good as ended. It was a foregone conclusion, that the great end for which he, and so many other great and good men of the Republic had for so many years been earnestly striving, would be an accomplished fact. They had not failed; they had stood firm; the victory which he had predicted six years before had come!

[He had said in his Springfield speech, of 1858: "We shall not fail; if we stand firm we shall not fail; wise counsels may accelerate, or mistakes delay, but sooner or later the Victory is sure to come."]

LINCOLN'S SECOND INAUGURATION

While the death of Slavery in America was decreed, as we have seen; yet, the sanguine anticipations of Mr. Lincoln, and other friends of Freedom, that such a decree, imperishably grafted into the Constitution, must at once end the Rebellion, and bring Peace with a restored Union, were not realized. The War went on. Grant was still holding Lee, at Petersburg, near Richmond, while Sherman's victorious Army was about entering upon a campaign from Savannah, up through the Carolinas.

During the previous Summer, efforts had been made, by Horace Greeley, and certain parties supposed to represent the Rebel authorities, to lay the ground-work for an early Peace and adjustment of the differences between the Government of the United States and the Rebels, but they miscarried. They led, however, to the publication of the following important conciliatory Presidential announcement:

"EXECUTIVE MANSION,

"WASHINGTON, July 18, 1864.

"To whom it may concern:

"Any proposition which embraces the restoration of Peace, the integrity of the whole Union, and the abandonment of Slavery, and which comes by and with an authority that can control the Armies now at War against the United States, will be received and considered by the Executive Government of the United States, and will be met by liberal terms on substantial and collateral points; and the bearer or bearers thereof shall have safe conduct both ways.

"(Signed) ABRAHAM LINCOLN."

About the same time, other efforts were being made, with a similar object in view, but which came to naught. The visit of Messrs. Jacques and Gilmore to the Rebel Capital on an informal Peace-errand was, at least, valuable in this, that it secured from the head and front of the armed

Conspiracy, Jefferson Davis himself, the following definite statement:
"I desire Peace as much as you do; I deplore bloodshed as much as you do; but I feel that not one drop of the blood shed in this War is on my hands. I can look up to my God and say this. I tried all in my power to avert this War. I saw it coming, and for twelve years I worked night and day to prevent it; but I could not. The North was mad and blind; it would not let us govern ourselves; and so the War came: and now it must go on till the last man of this generation falls in his tracks, and his children seize his musket and fight our battle, unless you acknowledge our right to self-government. We are not fighting for Slavery. We are fighting for INDEPENDENCE; and that, or EXTERMINATION, we WILL have."

[The Nation, July 2, 1885, contained the following remarks, which may be pertinently quoted in support of this authoritative statement that the South was "not fighting for Slavery," but for Independence—that is to say: for Power, and what would flow from it.]

["The Charleston News and Courier a fortnight ago remarked that 'not more than one Southern soldier in ten or fifteen was a Slaveholder, or had any interest in Slave Property.' The Laurensville Herald disputed the statement, and declared that 'the Southern Army was really an Army of Slaveholders and the sons of Slaveholders.' The Charleston paper stands by its original position, and cites figures which are conclusive. The Military population of the eleven States which seceded, according to the census of 1860, was 1,064,193. The entire number of Slaveholders in the Country at the same time was 383,637, but of these 77,335 lived in the Border States, so that the number in the Seceding States was only 306,302. Most of the small Slaveholders, however, were not Slave-owners, but Slave hirers, and Mr. De Bow, the statistician who supervised the census of 1850, estimated that but little over half the holders were actually owners. The proportion of owners diminished between 1850 and 1860, and the News and Courier thinks that there were not more than 150,000 Slave-owners in the Confederate States when the War broke out. This would be one owner to every seven White males between eighteen and forty-five; but as many of the owners were women, and many of the men were relieved from Military service, the Charleston paper is confirmed in its original opinion that there were ten men in the Southern Army who were not Slave-owners for every soldier who had Slaves of his own."]

And when these self-constituted Peace-delegates had fulfilled the duty which their zeal had impelled them to perform, and were taking their leave of the Rebel chieftain, Jefferson Davis added:
"Say to Mr. Lincoln, from me, that I shall at any time be pleased to receive proposals for PEACE on the basis of our INDEPENDENCE. It will be useless to approach me with any other."

Thus the lines had been definitely and distinctly drawn, on both sides. The issue of Slavery became admittedly, as between the Government and the Rebels, a dead one. The great cardinal issue was now clearly seen and authoritatively admitted to be, "the integrity of the whole Union" on the one side, and on the other, "Independence of a part of it." These precise declarations did great good to the Union Cause in the North, and not only helped the triumphant re-election of Mr. Lincoln, but also contributed to weaken the position of the Northern advocates of Slavery, and to bring about, as we have seen, the extinction of that inherited National curse, by Constitutional Amendment.

During January, of 1865, Francis P. Blair having been permitted to pass both the Union and Rebel Army lines, showed to Mr. Lincoln a letter, written to the former, by Jefferson Davis—and which the latter had authorized him to read to the President—stating that he had always been, and was still, ready to send or to receive Commissioners "to enter into a Conference, with a view to secure Peace to the two Countries." On the 18th of that month, purposing to having it shown to Jefferson Davis, Mr. Lincoln wrote to Mr. Blair a letter in which, after referring to Mr. Davis, he said: "You may say to him that I have constantly been, am now, and shall continue, ready to receive any agent whom he, or any other influential person now resisting the National Authority, may informally send to me, with the view of securing Peace to the People of our common Country." On the 21st of January, Mr. Blair was again in Richmond; and Mr. Davis had read and retained Mr. Lincoln's letter to Blair, who specifically drew the Rebel chieftain's attention to the fact that "the part about 'our common Country' related to the part of Mr. Davis's letter about 'the two Countries,' to which Mr. Davis replied that he so understood it." Yet subsequently, he sent Messrs. Alexander H. Stephens, R. M. T. Hunter, and John A. Campbell as Commissioners, with instructions, (January 28, 1865,) which, after setting forth the language of Mr. Lincoln's letter, proceeded strangely enough to say: "In conformity with the letter of Mr. Lincoln, of which the foregoing is a copy, you are to proceed to Washington city for informal Conference with him upon the issues involved in the existing War, and for the purpose of securing Peace to the two Countries!" The Commissioners themselves stated in writing that "The substantial object to be obtained by the informal Conference is, to ascertain upon what terms the existing War can be terminated honorably. * * * Our earnest desire is, that a just and honorable Peace may be agreed upon, and we are prepared to receive or to submit propositions which may, possibly, lead to the attainment of that end." In consequence of this peculiarly "mixed" overture, the President sent Secretary Seward to Fortress Monroe, to informally confer with the parties, specifically instructing him to "make known to them that three things are indispensable, to wit:

"1. The restoration of the National Authority throughout all the States.

"2. No receding, by the Executive of the United States, on the Slavery question, from the position assumed thereon in the late Annual Message to Congress, and in preceding documents.

"3. No cessation of hostilities short of an end of the War and the disbanding of all forces hostile to the Government."

Mr. Lincoln also instructed the Secretary to "inform them that all propositions of theirs, not inconsistent with the above, will be considered and passed upon in a spirit of sincere liberality;" to "hear all they may choose to say, and report it" to him, and not to "assume to definitely consummate anything." Subsequently, the President, in consequence of a dispatch from General Grant to Secretary Stanton, decided to go himself to Fortress Monroe.

Following is the dispatch:

[In Cipher]

OFFICE UNITED STATES MILITARY TELEGRAPH. WAR DEPARTMENT.

"The following telegram received at Washington, 4.35 A.M.,

February 2, 1865. From City Point, Va.,

February 1, 10.30 P.M., 1865

"Now that the interview between Major Eckert, under his written instructions, and Mr. Stephens and party has ended, I will state confidentially, but not officially, to become a matter of record, that I am convinced, upon conversation with Messrs. Stephens and Hunter, that their intentions are good and their desire sincere to restore Peace and Union. I have not felt myself at liberty to express, even, views of my own, or to account for my reticency. This has placed me in an awkward position, which I could have avoided by not seeing them in the first instance. I fear now their going back without any expression from any one in authority will have a bad influence. At the same time I recognize the difficulties in the way of receiving these informal Commissioners at this time, and do not know what to recommend. I am sorry, however, that Mr. Lincoln cannot have an interview with the two named in this dispatch, if not all three now within our lines. Their letter to me was all that the President's instructions contemplated to secure their safe conduct, if they had used the same language to Major Eckert.

"U. S. GRANT,

"Lieutenant General.

"Hon. EDWIN M. STANTON,

"Secretary of War."

Mr. Stephens is stated by a Georgia paper to have repeated the following characteristic anecdote of what occurred during the interview. "The three Southern gentlemen met Mr. Lincoln and Mr. Seward, and after some preliminary remarks, the subject of Peace was opened. Mr. Stephens, well aware that one who asks much may get more than he who confesses to humble wishes at the outset, urged the claims of his Section with that skill and address for which the Northern papers have given him credit. Mr. Lincoln, holding the vantage ground of conscious power, was, however, perfectly frank, and submitted his views almost in the form of an argument. * * * Davis had, on this occasion, as on that of Mr. Stephens's visit to Washington, made it a condition that no Conference should be had unless his rank as Commander or President should first be recognized. Mr. Lincoln declared that the only ground on which he could rest the justice of War—either with his own people, or with foreign powers—was that it was not a War for conquest, for that the States had never been separated from the Union. Consequently, he could not recognize another Government inside of the one of which he alone was President; nor admit the separate Independence of States that were yet a part of the Union. 'That' said he 'would be doing what you have so long asked Europe to do in vain, and be resigning the only thing the Armies of the Union have been fighting for.' Mr. Hunter made a long reply to this, insisting that the recognition of Davis's power to make a Treaty was the first and indispensable step to Peace, and referred to the correspondence between King Charles I., and his Parliament, as a trustworthy precedent of a Constitutional ruler treating with Rebels. Mr. Lincoln's face then wore that indescribable expression which generally preceded his hardest hits, and he remarked: 'Upon questions of history I must refer you to Mr. Seward, for he is posted in such things, and I don't pretend to be bright. My only distinct recollection of the matter is that Charles lost his head,' That settled Mr. Hunter for a while." Arnold's Lincoln, p. 400.

On the night of February 2nd, Mr. Lincoln reached Hampton Roads, and joined Secretary Seward on board a steamer anchored off the shore. The next morning, from another steamer, similarly anchored, Messrs. Stephens, Hunter, and Campbell were brought aboard the President's steamer and a Conference with the President and Secretary of several hours' duration was the result. Mr. Lincoln's own statement of what transpired was in these words:

"No question of preliminaries to the meeting was then and there made or mentioned. No other person was present; no papers were exchanged or produced; and it was, in advance, agreed that the conversation was to be informal and verbal merely. On our part, the whole substance of the instructions to the Secretary of State, hereinbefore recited, was stated and insisted upon, and nothing was said inconsistent therewith; while, by the other party, it was not said that in any event or on any condition, they ever would consent to Re-union; and yet they equally omitted to declare that they never would so consent. They seemed to desire a postponement of that question, and the adoption of some other course first, which, as some of them seemed to argue, might or might not lead to Reunion; but which course, we thought, would amount to an indefinite postponement. The Conference ended without result."

In his communication to the Rebel Congress at Richmond, February 6. 1865, Jefferson Davis, after mentioning his appointment of Messrs. Stephens, Hunter and Campbell, for the purpose stated, proceeded to say: "I herewith transmit, for the information of Congress, the report of the eminent citizens above named, showing that the Enemy refused to enter into negotiations with the Confederate States, or any one of them separately, or to give to our people any other terms or guarantees than those which the conqueror may grant, or to permit us to have Peace on any other basis than our unconditional submission to their rule, coupled with the acceptance of their recent legislation on the subject of the relations between the White and Black population of each State."

On the 5th and 9th of February, public meetings were held at Richmond, in connection with these Peace negotiations. At the first, Jefferson Davis made a speech in which the Richmond Dispatch reported him as emphatically asserting that no conditions of Peace "save the Independence of the Confederacy could ever receive his sanction. He doubted not that victory would yet crown our labors, * * * and sooner than we should ever be united again he would be willing to yield up everything he had on Earth, and if it were possible would sacrifice a thousand lives before he would succumb." Thereupon the meeting of Rebels passed resolutions "spurning" Mr. Lincoln's terms "with the indignation due to so gross an insult;" declared that the circumstances connected with his offer could only "add to the outrage and stamp it as a designed and premeditated indignity" offered to them; and invoking "the aid of Almighty God" to carry out their "resolve to maintain" their "Liberties and Independence"—to which, said they, "we mutually pledge our lives, our fortunes, and our sacred honor." So too, at the second of these meetings, presided over by R. M. T. Hunter, and addressed by the Rebel Secretary Judah P. Benjamin, resolutions were adopted amid "wild and long continued cheering," one of which stated that they would "never lay down" their "arms until" their "Independence" had "been won," while another declared a full confidence in the sufficiency of their resources to "conduct the War successfully and to that issue," and invoked "the People, in the name of the holiest of all causes, to spare neither their blood nor their treasure in its maintenance and support."

As during these Peace negotiations, General Grant, by express direction of President Lincoln, had not changed, hindered, nor delayed, any of his "Military movements or plans," so, now that the negotiations had failed, those Military movements were pressed more strenuously than ever.

[The main object of this Conference on the part of the Rebels was to secure an immediate truce, or breathing spell, during which they could get themselves in better condition for continuing the War. Indeed a portion of Mr. Seward's letter of Feb. 7, 1865, to Mr. Adams, our Minister at the Court of St. James, giving him an account of the Conference with the party of Insurgent Commissioners, would not alone indicate this, but also that it was proposed by that "Insurgent party," that both sides, during the time they would thus cease to fight one another, might profitably combine their forces to drive the French invaders out of Mexico and annex that valuable country. At least, the following passage in that letter will bear that construction:

"What the Insurgent party seemed chiefly to favor was a postponement of the question of separation, upon which the War is waged, and a mutual direction of efforts of the Government, as well as those of the Insurgents, to some extrinsic policy or scheme for a season, during which passions might be expected to subside, and the Armies be reduced, and trade and intercourse between the People of both Sections resumed. It was suggested by them that through such postponements we might now have immediate Peace, with some not very certain prospect of an ultimate satisfactory adjustment of political relations between this Government, and the States, Section, or People, now engaged in conflict with it."

For the whole of this letter see McPherson's History of the Rebellion, p. 570.]

Fort Fisher, North Carolina, had already been captured by a combined Military and Naval attack of the Union forces under General Terry and Admiral Porter; and Sherman's Army was now victoriously advancing from Savannah, Georgia, Northwardly through South Carolina. On the 17th of February, Columbia, the capital of the latter State, surrendered, and, the day following, Charleston was evacuated, and its defenses, including historic Fort Sumter, were once more under that glorious old flag of the Union which four years before had been driven away, by shot and shell and flame, amid the frantic exultations of the temporarily successful armed Conspirators of South Carolina. On the 22nd of February, General Schofield, who had been sent by Grant with his 23rd Corps, by water, to form a junction with Terry's troops about Fort Fisher, and capture Wilmington, North Carolina, had also accomplished his purpose successfully.

The Rebel Cause now began to look pretty desperate, even to Rebel eyes.

[Hundreds of Rebels were now deserting from Lee's Armies about Richmond, every night, owing partly to despondency. "These desertions," wrote Lee, on the 24th February, "have a very bad effect upon the troops who remain, and give rise to painful apprehensions." Another cause was the lack of food and clothing. Says Badeau (Military History of Ulysses S. Grant, vol. iii., p. 399): "On the 8th of January, Lee wrote to the Rebel Government that the entire Right Wing of his Army had been in line for three days and nights, in the most inclement weather of the season. 'Under these circumstances,' he said, 'heightened by assaults and fire of the Enemy, some of the men had been without meat for three days, and all were suffering from reduced rations and scant clothing. Colonel Cole, chief commissary, reports that he has not a pound of meat at his disposal. If some change is not made, and the commissary department reorganized, I apprehend dire results. The physical strength of the men, if their courage survives, must fail under this treatment. Our Cavalry has to be dispersed for want of forage. Fitz Lee's and Lomax's Divisions are scattered because supplies cannot be transported where their services are required. I had to bring Fitz Lee's Division sixty miles Sunday night, to get them in position. Taking these facts in connection with the paucity of our numbers, you must not be surprised if calamity befalls us.'" Badeau's (Grant, vol. iii., p. 401,)]

Toward the end of February, the Rebel General Longstreet having requested an interview with General Ord "to arrange for the exchange of citizen prisoners, and prisoners of war, improperly captured," General Grant authorized General Ord to hold such interview t and "to arrange definitely for such as were confined in his department, arrangements for all others to be submitted for approval." In the course of that interview "a general conversation ensued on the subject of the War," when it would seem that Longstreet suggested the idea of a composition of the questions at issue, and Peace between the United States and the Rebels, by means of a Military Convention. It is quite probable that this idea originated with Jefferson Davis, as a dernier resort; for Longstreet appears to have communicated directly with Davis concerning his interview or "interviews" with Ord. On the 28th of February, 1865 the Rebel Chief wrote to Lee, as follows:

"RICHMOND, VA., February 28.

"Gen. R. E. LEE, Commanding, etc.,

"GENERAL: You will learn by the letter of General Longstreet the result of his second interview with General Ord. The points as to whether yourself or General Grant should invite the other to a Conference is not worth discussing. If you think the statements of General Ord render it probably useful that the Conference suggested should be had, you will proceed as you may prefer, and are clothed with all the supplemental authority you may need in the consideration of any proposition for a Military Convention, or the appointment of a Commissioner to enter into such an arrangement as will cause at least temporary suspension of hostilities.

"Very truly yours

"JEFFERSON DAVIS."

Thereupon General Lee wrote, and sent to General Grant, the following communication:

"HEADQUARTERS C. S. ARMIES, March 2, 1865.
"Lieut. Gen. U. S. GRANT,
"Commanding United States Armies:
"GENERAL: Lieut.-Gen. Longstreet has informed me that, in a recent conversation between himself and Maj.-Gen. Ord, as to the possibility of arriving at a satisfactory adjustment of the present unhappy difficulties by means of a Military Convention, General Ord stated that if I desired to have an interview with you on the subject, you would not decline, provided I had authority to act. Sincerely desirous to leave nothing untried which may put an end to the calamities of War, I propose to meet you at such convenient time and place as you may designate, with the hope that, upon an interchange of views, it may be found practicable to submit the subjects of controversy between the belligerents to a Convention of the kind mentioned.

"In such event, I am authorized to do whatever the result of the proposed interview may render necessary or advisable. Should you accede to this proposition, I would suggest that, if agreeable to you, we meet at the place selected by Generals Ord and Longstreet, for the interview, at 11 A.M., on Monday next.

"Very respectfully your obedient servant,
"R. E. LEE, General."

Upon receipt of this letter, General Grant sent a telegraphic dispatch to Secretary Stanton, informing him of Lee's proposition. It reached the Secretary of War just before midnight of March 3rd. He, and the other members of the Cabinet were with the President, in the latter's room at the Capitol, whither they had gone on this, the last, night of the last Session of the Thirty-Eighth Congress, the Cabinet to advise, and the President to act, upon bills submitted to him for approval. The Secretary, after reading the dispatch, handed it to Mr. Lincoln. The latter read and thought over it briefly, and then himself wrote the following reply:

"WASHINGTON, March, 3, 1865, 12 P.M.
"LIEUTENANT GENERAL GRANT: The President directs me to say to you that he wishes you to have no Conference with General Lee, unless it be for the capitulation of General Lee's Army, or on some other minor and purely Military matter. He instructs me to say to you that you are not to decide, discuss, or confer upon any political question. Such questions the President holds in his own hands, and will submit them to no Military Conferences or Conventions. Meanwhile you are to press to the utmost your Military advantages.

"EDWIN M. STANTON,
"Secretary of War."

General Grant received this dispatch, on the day following, and at once wrote and sent to General Lee a communication in which, after referring to the subject of the exchange of prisoners, he said: "In regard to meeting you on the 6th inst., I would state that—I have no authority to accede to your proposition for a Conference on the subject proposed. Such authority is vested in the President of the United States alone. General Ord could only have meant that I would not refuse an interview on any subject on which I have a right to act; which, of course, would be such as are purely of a Military character, and on the subject of exchange, which has been entrusted to me."

Thus perished the last reasonable hope entertained by the Rebel Chieftains to ward off the inevitable and mortal blow that was about to smite their Cause.

The 4th of March, 1865, had come. The Thirty-Eighth Congress was no more. Mr. Lincoln was about to be inaugurated, for a second term, as President of the United States. The previous night had been vexed with a stormy snow-fall. The morning had also been stormy and rainy. By mid-day, however, as if to mark the event auspiciously, the skies cleared and the sun shone gloriously upon the thousands and tens of thousands who had come to Washington, to witness the second Inauguration of him whom the people had now, long since, learned to affectionately term "Father Abraham"—of him who had become the veritable Father of his People. As the President left the White House, to join the grand procession to the Capitol, a brilliant meteor shot athwart the heavens, above his head. At the time, the superstitious thought it an Omen of triumph—of coming Peace— but in the sad after-days when armed Rebellion had ceased and Peace had come, it was remembered, with a shudder, as a portent of ill. When, at last, Mr. Lincoln stood, with bared head, upon the platform at the eastern portico of the Capitol, where four years before, he had made his vows before the People, under such very different circumstances and surroundings, the contrast between that time and this—and all the terrible and eventful history of the interim—could not fail to present itself to every mind of all those congregated, whether upon the platform among the gorgeously costumed foreign diplomats, the full-uniformed Military and Naval officers of the United States, and the more soberly-clad statesmen and Civic and Judicial functionaries of the Land, or in the vast and indiscriminate mass of the enthusiastic people in front and on both sides of it. As Chief Justice Chase administered the oath, and Abraham Lincoln, in view of all the people, reverently bowed his head and kissed the open Bible, at a passage in Isaiah (27th and 28th verses of the 5th Chapter) which it was thought "admonished him to be on his guard, and not to relax at all, in his efforts," the people, whose first cheers of welcome had been stayed by the President's uplifted hand, broke forth in a tumult of cheering, until again hushed by the clear, strong, even voice of the President, as he delivered that second Inaugural Address, whose touching tenderness, religious resignation, and Christian charity, were clad in these imperishable words:

"FELLOW COUNTRYMEN: At this second appearing to take the Oath of the Presidential office, there is less occasion for an extended address than there was at the first. Then, a statement, somewhat in detail, of a course to be pursued, seemed fitting and proper. Now, at the expiration of four years, during which public declarations have been constantly called forth on every point and phase of the great contest which still absorbs the attention and engrosses the energy of the Nation, little that is new could be presented. The progress of our Arms, upon which all else depends, is as well known to the public as to myself; and it is, I trust, reasonably satisfactory and encouraging to all. With high hope for the future, no prediction in regard to it is ventured.

"On the occasion corresponding to this, four years ago, all thoughts were anxiously directed to an impending Civil War. All dreaded it—all sought to avert it. While the Inaugural Address was being delivered from this place, devoted altogether to saving the Union without War, Insurgent agents were in the city, seeking to destroy it without War—seeking to dissolve the Union, and divide the effects, by negotiation. Both parties deprecated War; but one of them would make War rather than let the Nation survive; and the other would accept War rather than let it perish—and the War came.

"One-eighth of the whole population were colored Slaves, not distributed generally over the Union, but localized in the Southern part of it. These Slaves constituted a peculiar and powerful interest. All knew that this interest was, somehow, the cause of the War. To strengthen, perpetuate and extend this interest was the object for which the Insurgents would rend the Union, even by War; while the Government claimed no right to do more than to restrict the territorial enlargement of it. Neither Party expected for the War the magnitude or the duration which it has already attained. Neither anticipated that the cause of the conflict might cease with, or even before, the conflict itself should cease. Each looked for an easier triumph, and a result less fundamental and astounding. Both read the same Bible, and pray to the same God; and each invokes His aid against the other. It may seem strange that any men should dare to ask a just God's assistance in wringing their bread from the sweat of other men's faces; but let us judge not, that we be not judged. The prayers of both could not be answered— that of neither has been answered fully. The Almighty has His own purposes. 'Woe unto the World because of offences! for it must needs be that offences come; but woe to that man by whom the offence cometh.' If we shall suppose that American Slavery is one of those offences which, in the providence of God, must needs come, but which, having continued through His appointed time, He now wills to remove, and that He gives to both North and South this terrible War, as the woe due to those by Whom the offence came, shall we discern therein any departure from those divine attributes which the believers in a living God always ascribe to Him? Fondly do we hope—fervently do we pray—that this mighty scourge of War may speedily pass away. Yet, if God wills that it continue until all the wealth piled by the bondman's two hundred and fifty years of unrequited toil shall be sunk, and until every drop of blood drawn with the lash shall be paid by another drawn with the sword, as was said three thousand years ago, so still it must be said, 'The judgments of the Lord are true and righteous altogether.'

"With malice toward none; with charity for all; with firmness in the right, as God gives us to see the right, let us strive on to finish the work we are in; to bind up the Nation's wounds, to care for him who shall have borne the battle, and for his widow, and his orphan—to do all which may achieve and cherish a just and a lasting Peace among ourselves, and with all Nations."

With utterances so just and fair, so firm and hopeful, so penitent and humble, so benignant and charitable, so mournfully tender and sweetly solemn, so full of the fervor of true piety and the very pathos of patriotism, small wonder is it that among those numberless thousands who, on this memorable occasion, gazed upon the tall, gaunt form of Abraham Lincoln, and heard his clear, sad voice, were some who almost imagined they saw the form and heard the voice of one of the great prophets and leaders of Israel; while others were more reminded of one of the Holy Apostles of the later Dispensation who preached the glorious Gospel "On Earth, Peace, good will toward Men," and received in the end the crown of Christian martyrdom. But not one soul of those present—unless his own felt such presentiment—dreamed for a moment that, all too soon, the light of those brave and kindly eyes was fated to go out in darkness, that sad voice to be hushed forever, that form to lie bleeding and dead, a martyred sacrifice indeed, upon the altar of his Country!

COLLAPSE OF THE ARMED CONSPIRACY

Meantime, Sherman's Armies were pressing along upward, toward Raleigh, from Columbia, marching through swamps and over quicksands and across swollen streams—cold, wet, hungry, tired—often up to their armpits in water, yet keeping their powder dry, and silencing opposing batteries or driving the Enemy, who doggedly retired before them, through the drenching rains which poured down unceasingly for days, and even weeks, at a time. On the 16th of March, 1865, a part of Sherman's Forces met the Enemy, under General Joe Johnston, at Averysboro, N. C., and forced him to retire. On the 19th and 20th of March, occurred the series of engagements, about Mill Creek and the Bentonville and Smithfield cross-roads, which culminated in the attack upon the Enemy, of the 21st of March, and his evacuation, that night, of his entire line of works, and retreat upon Smithfield. This was known as the Battle of Bentonville, and was the last battle fought between the rival Forces under Sherman and Johnston. The Armies of Sherman, now swollen by having formed a junction with the troops under Schofield and Terry, which had come from Newbern and Wilmington, went into camp at Goldsboro, North Carolina, to await the rebuilding of the railroads from those two points on the coast, and the arrival of badly needed clothing, provision, and other supplies, after which the march would be resumed to Burksville, Virginia. By the 25th of March, the railroad from Newbern was in running order, and General Sherman, leaving General Schofield in command of his eighty thousand troops, went to Newbern and Morehead City, and thence by steamer to City Point, for a personal interview with General Grant. On the same day, Lee made a desperate but useless assault, with twenty thousand (of his seventy thousand) men upon Fort Stedman—a portion of Grant's works in front of Petersburg. On the 27th, President Lincoln reached City Point, on the

27

James River, in the steamer "Ocean Queen." Sherman reached City Point the same day, and, after meeting the General-in-Chief, Grant took him on board the "Ocean Queen" to see the President. Together they explained to Mr. Lincoln the Military situation, during the "hour or more" they were with him. Of this interview with Mr. Lincoln, General Sherman afterwards wrote: "General Grant and I explained to him that my next move from Goldsboro would bring my Army, increased to eighty thousand men by Schofield's and Terry's reinforcements, in close communication with General Grant's Army, then investing Lee in Richmond, and that unless Lee could effect his escape, and make junction with Johnston in North Carolina, he would soon be shut up in Richmond with no possibility of supplies, and would have to surrender. Mr. Lincoln was extremely interested in this view of the case, and when we explained that Lee's only chance was to escape, join Johnston, and, being then between me in North Carolina, and Grant in Virginia, could choose which to fight. Mr. Lincoln seemed unusually impressed with this; but General Grant explained that, at the very moment of our conversation, General Sheridan was passing his Cavalry across James River, from the North to the South; that he would, with this Cavalry, so extend his left below Petersburg as to meet the South Shore Road; and that if Lee should 'let go' his fortified lines, he (Grant) would follow him so close that he could not possibly fall on me alone in North Carolina. I, in like manner, expressed the fullest confidence that my Army in North Carolina was willing to cope with Lee and Johnston combined, till Grant could come up. But we both agreed that one more bloody battle was likely to occur before the close of the War. Mr. Lincoln * * * more than once exclaimed: 'Must more blood be shed? Cannot this last bloody battle be avoided?' We explained that we had to presume that General Lee was a real general; that he must see that Johnston alone was no barrier to my progress; and that if my Army of eighty thousand veterans should reach Burksville, he was lost in Richmond; and that we were forced to believe he would not await that inevitable conclusion, but make one more desperate effort."

President Lincoln's intense anxiety caused him to remain at City Point, from this time forth, almost until the end—receiving from General Grant, when absent, at the immediate front, frequent dispatches, which, as fast as received and read, he transmitted to the Secretary of War, at Washington. Grant had already given general instructions to Major-Generals Meade, Ord, and Sheridan, for the closing movements of his immediate Forces, against Lee and his lines of supply and possible retreat. He saw that the time had come for which he had so long waited, and he now felt "like ending the matter." On the morning of the 29th of March—preliminary dispositions having been executed—the movements began. That night, Grant wrote to Sheridan, who was at Dinwiddie Court House, with his ten thousand Cavalry: "Our line is now unbroken from the Appomattox to Dinwiddie. * * * I feel now like ending the matter, if it is possible to do so, before going back. * * * In the morning, push around the Enemy, if you can, and get on his right rear. * * * We will all act together as one Army, until it is seen what can be done with the Enemy." The rain fell all that night in torrents. The face of the country, where forests, swamps, and quicksands alternated in presenting apparently insuperable obstacles to immediate advance, was very discouraging next morning, but Sheridan's heart was gladdened by orders to seize Five Forks.

On the 31st, the Battle of Dinwiddie Court House occurred—the Enemy attacking Sheridan and Warren with a largely superior force. During the night, Sheridan was reinforced with the Fifth Corps, and other troops. On April 1st, Sheridan fought, and won, the glorious Battle of Five Forks, against this detached Rebel force, and, besides capturing 6,000 prisoners and six pieces of artillery, dispersed the rest to the North and West, away from the balance of Lee's Army. That night, after Grant received the news of this victory, he went into his tent, wrote a dispatch, sent it by an orderly, and returning to the fire outside his tent, calmly said: "I have ordered an immediate assault along the lines." This was afterward modified to an attack at three points, on the Petersburg works, at 4 o'clock in the morning—a terrific bombardment, however, to be kept up all night. Grant also sent more reinforcements to Sheridan. On the morning of April 2nd, the assault was made, and the Enemy's works were gallantly carried, while Sheridan was coming up to the West of Petersburg.

The Rebel Chieftain Lee, when his works were stormed and carried, is said to have exclaimed: "It has happened as I thought; the lines have been stretched until they broke." At 10.30 A. M. he telegraphed to Jefferson Davis: "My lines are broken in three places. Richmond must be evacuated this evening." This dispatch of Parke, Ord on Wright's left, Humphreys on Ord's left and Warren on Humphrey's left—Sheridan being to the rear and left of Warren, reached Davis, while at church. All present felt, as he retired, that the end of the Rebellion had come. At 10.40 A. M. Lee reported further: "I see no prospect of doing more than holding our position here till night. I am not certain that I can do that. If I can, I shall withdraw tonight, North of the Appomattox, and if possible, it will be better to withdraw the whole line to-night from James river. * * * Our only chance of concentrating our Forces is to do so near Danville railroad, which I shall endeavor to do at once. I advise that all preparations be made for leaving Richmond to-night. I will advise you later, according to circumstances. "At 7 o'clock P. M. Lee again communicated to the Rebel Secretary of War this information: "It is absolutely necessary that we should abandon our position to-night, or run the risk of being cut off in the morning. I have given all the orders to officers on both sides of the river, and have taken every precaution that I can to make the movement successful. It will be a difficult operation, but I hope not impracticable. Please give all orders that you find necessary, in and about Richmond. The troops will all be directed to Amelia Court House." This was the last dispatch sent by Lee to the Rebel Government.

On the 3rd of April, Petersburg and Richmond were evacuated, and again under the Union flag, while Grant's immediate Forces were pressing forward to cut off the retreat of Lee, upon Amelia Court House and Danville, in an effort to form a junction with Johnston. On the 6th, the important Battle of Sailor's Creek, Va., was fought and won by Sheridan. On the evening of the 7th, at the Farmville hotel, where Lee had slept the night before, Grant, after sending dispatches to Sheridan at Prospect Station, Ord at Prince Edward's Court House, and Mead at Rice Station, wrote the following letter to Lee:

"FARMVILLE, April 7th, 1865.

"GENERAL: The results of the last week must convince you of the hopelessness of further resistance, on the part of the Army of Northern Virginia, in this struggle. I feel that it is so, and regard it as my duty to shift from myself the responsibility of any further effusion of blood, by asking of you the surrender of that portion of the Confederate States' army known as the Army of Northern Virginia.

"U. S. GRANT,

"Lieutenant-General."

Lee, however, in replying to this demand, and in subsequent correspondence, seemed to be unable to see "the hopelessness of further resistance." He thought "the emergency had not yet come." Hence, Grant decided to so press and harass him, as to bring the emergency along quickly. Accordingly, by the night of the 8th of April, Sheridan with his Cavalry had completely headed Lee off, at Appomattox Court House. By morning, Ord's forces had reached Sheridan, and were in line behind him. Two Corps of the Army of the Potomac, under Meade, were also, by this time, close on the Enemy's rear. And now the harassed Enemy, conscious that his rear was threatened, and seeing only Cavalry in his front, through which to fight his way, advanced to the attack. The dismounted Cavalry of Sheridan contested the advance, in order to give Ord and Griffin as much time as possible to form, then, mounting and moving rapidly aside, they suddenly uncovered, to the charging Rebels, Ord's impenetrable barrier of Infantry, advancing upon them at a double-quick! At the same time that this appalling sight staggered them, and rolled them back in despair, they became aware that Sheridan's impetuous Cavalry, now mounted, were hovering on their left flank, evidently about to charge!

Lee at once concluded that the emergency "had now come," and sent, both to Sheridan and Meade, a flag of truce, asking that hostilities cease, pending negotiations for a surrender—having also requested of Grant an audience with a view to such surrender. That afternoon the two great rival Military Chieftains met by appointment in the plain little farm-house of one McLean—Lee dressed in his best full-dress uniform and sword, Grant in a uniform soiled and dusty, and without any sword—and, after a few preliminary words, as to the terms proposed by Grant, the latter sat down to the table, and wrote the following:

"APPOMATTOX COURT HOUSE,

"VIRGINIA, April 9, 1865.

"GENERAL: In accordance with the substance of my letter to you of the 8th instant, I propose to receive the surrender of the Army of Northern Virginia on the following terms, to wit: Rolls of all the officers and men to be made in duplicate, one copy to be given to an officer to be designated by me, the other to be retained by such officer or officers as you may designate. The officers to give their individual paroles not to take up arms against the Government of the United States, until properly exchanged; and each company or regimental commander to sign a like parole for the men of their commands. The arms, artillery, and public property to be parked and stacked, and turned over to the officers appointed by me to receive them. This will not embrace the side-arms of the officers nor their private horses or baggage. This done, each officer and man will be allowed to return to his home, not to be disturbed by United States authority so long as they observe their paroles and the laws in force where they may reside.

"U. S. GRANT,

"Lieutenant-General.

"General R. E. LEE."

After some further conversation, in which Grant intimated that his officers receiving paroles would be instructed to "allow the Cavalry and Artillery men to retain their horses, and take them home to work their little farms"—a kindness which Lee said, would "have the best possible effect," the latter wrote his surrender in the following words:

"HEAD-QUARTERS, ARMY OF NORTHERN VIRGINIA, April 9, 1865.

"GENERAL: I received your letter of this date containing the terms of the surrender of the Army of Northern Virginia, as proposed by you. As they are substantially the same as those expressed in your letter of the 8th instant, they are accepted. I will proceed to designate the proper officers to carry the stipulations into effect. "R. E. LEE, General.

"Lieutenant-General U. S. GRANT."

Before parting, Lee told Grant that his men were starving; and Grant at once ordered 25,000 rations to be issued to the surrendered Rebels—and then the Rebel Chieftain, shaking hands with the Victor, rode away to his conquered legions. It was 4.30 P.M. when Grant, on his way to his own headquarters, now with Sheridan's command, dismounted from his horse, and sitting on a stone by the roadside, wrote the following dispatch:

"Hon. E. M. STANTON,

Secretary of War, Washington.

"General Lee surrendered the Army of Northern Virginia this afternoon on terms proposed by myself. The accompanying additional correspondence will show the conditions fully.

"U. S. GRANT, Lieutenant General."

Meanwhile on the 5th of April, Grant, who had kept Sherman, as well as Sheridan, advised of his main movements, had also ordered the former to press Johnston's Army as he was pressing Lee, so as, between them, they might "push on, and finish the job." In accordance with this order, Sherman's Forces advanced toward Smithfield, and, Johnston having rapidly retreated before them, entered Raleigh, North Carolina, on the 13th. The 14th of April, brought the news of the surrender of Lee to Grant, and the same day a correspondence was opened between Sherman and Johnston, looking to the surrender of the latter's Army—terms for which were actually agreed upon, subject, however, to approval of Sherman's superiors. Those terms, however, being considered unsatisfactory, were promptly disapproved, and similar terms to those allowed to Lee's Army, were substituted, and agreed to, the actual surrender taking place April 26th, near Durham, North Carolina. On the 21st, Macon, Georgia, with 12,000 Rebel Militia, and sixty guns, was surrendered to Wilson's Cavalry-command, by General Howell Cobb. On the 4th of May, General Richard Taylor surrendered all the armed Rebel troops, East of the Mississippi river; and on the 26th of May, General Kirby Smith surrendered all of them, West of that river.

On that day, organized, armed Rebellion against the United States ceased, and became a thing of the past. It had been conquered, stamped out, and extinguished, while its civic head, Jefferson Davis, captured May 11th, at Irwinsville, Georgia, while attempting to escape, was, with other leading Rebels, a prisoner in a Union fort. Four years of armed Rebellion had been enough for them. They were absolutely sick of it. And the magnanimity of the terms given them by Grant, completed their subjugation. "The wisdom of his course," says Badeau, "was proved by the haste which the Rebels made to yield everything they had fought for. They were ready not only to give up their arms, but literally to implore forgiveness of the Government. They acquiesced in the abolition of Slavery. They abandoned the heresy of Secession, and waited to learn what else their conquerors would dictate. They dreamed not of political power. They only asked to be let live quietly under the flag they had outraged, and attempt in some degree to rebuild their shattered fortunes. The greatest General of the Rebellion asked for pardon."

ASSASSINATION

But while some of the great Military events alluded to in the preceding Chapter, had been transpiring at the theatre of War, something else had happened at the National Capital, so momentous, so atrocious, so execrable, that it was with difficulty the victorious soldiers of the Union, when they first heard the news, could be restrained from turning upon the then remaining armed Rebels, and annihilating them in their righteous fury.

Let us go back, for a moment, to President Lincoln, whom we left on board the Ocean Queen, at City Point, toward the end of March and the beginning of April, receiving dispatches from Grant, who was victoriously engaged at the front. On the very day that Richmond fell—April 4th—President Lincoln, with his little son "Tad," Admiral Porter, and others, visited the burning city, and held a reception in the parlors of the Mansion which had now, for so many years, been occupied by the Chief Conspirator, Jefferson Davis, and which had been precipitately abandoned when the flight of that Arch-Rebel and his "Cabinet" commenced. On the 6th, the President, accompanied by his wife, Vice-President Johnson, and others from Washington, again visited Richmond, and received distinguished Virginians, to whom he addressed words of wisdom and patriotism.

["On this occasion," says Arnold, "he was called upon by several prominent citizens of Virginia, anxious to learn what the policy of the Government towards them would be. Without committing himself to specific details, he satisfied them that his policy would be magnanimous, forgiving, and generous. He told these Virginians they must learn loyalty and devotion to the Nation. They need not love Virginia less, but they must love the Republic more."]

On the 9th of April, he returned to Washington, and the same day—his last Sunday on Earth—came the grand and glorious news of Lee's surrender.

On the Wednesday evening following, he made a lengthy speech, at the White House, to the great crowd that had assembled about it, to congratulate him, and the Nation, upon the downfall of Rebellion. His first thought in that speech, was of gratitude to God. His second, to put himself in the background, and to give all the credit of Union Military success, to those who, under God, had achieved it. Said he: "We meet this evening, not in sorrow, but in gladness of heart. The evacuation of Petersburg and Richmond, and the surrender of the principal Insurgent Army, give hope of a righteous and speedy Peace, whose joyous expression cannot be restrained. In the midst of this, however, He from whom all blessings flow, must not be forgotten. A Call for a National Thanksgiving is being prepared, and will be duly promulgated. Nor must those whose harder part gives us the cause of rejoicing, be overlooked. Their honors must not be parcelled out with others. I myself was near the front, and had the high pleasure of transmitting much of the good news to you; but no part of the honor, for plan or execution, is mine. To General Grant, his skilful officers and brave men, all belongs."

This speech was almost entirely devoted to the subject of reconstruction of the States lately in Rebellion, and to an argument in favor of the Reconstruction policy, under which a new and loyal government had been formed for the State of Louisiana. "Some twelve thousand voters in the heretofore Slave State of Louisiana," said he, "have sworn allegiance to the Union, assumed to be the rightful political power of the State, held elections, organized a State government, adopted a Free State Constitution, giving the benefit of public schools equally to Black and White, and empowering the Legislature to confer the elective franchise upon the colored man. Their Legislature has already voted to ratify the Constitutional Amendment recently passed by Congress, abolishing Slavery throughout the Nation. These twelve thousand persons are thus fully committed to the Union, and to perpetual Freedom in the State; committed to the very things, and nearly all the things, the Nation wants; and they ask the Nation's recognition and its assistance to make good that committal. Now, if we reject and spurn them, we do our utmost to disorganize and disperse them. We, in effect, say to the White men, 'You are worthless, or worse; we will neither help you, nor be helped by you.' To the Blacks we say, 'This cup of Liberty which these, your old masters, hold to your lips, we will dash from you and leave you to the chances of gathering the spilled and scattered contents in some vague and undefined when, where, and how.' If this course, discouraging and paralyzing both White and Black, has any tendency to bring Louisiana into proper practical relations with the Union, I have, so far, been unable to perceive it. If, on the contrary, we recognize and sustain the new government of Louisiana, the converse of all this is made true."

While, however, Mr. Lincoln thus upheld and defended this Louisiana plan of reconstruction, yet he conceded that in applying it to other States, with their varying conditions, "no exclusive and inflexible plan can safely be prescribed as to details and collaterals." The entire speech shows the greatest solicitude to make no mistake necessitating backward steps, and consequent delay in reconstructing the Rebel States into Loyal ones; and especially anxious was he, in this, his last public utterance, touching the outcome of his great life-work, Emancipation. "If," said he, "we reject Louisiana, we also reject one vote in favor of the proposed Amendment to the National Constitution. To meet this proposition it has been argued that no more than three-fourths of those States which have not attempted Secession are necessary to validly ratify the Amendment. I do not commit myself against this further than to say that such a ratification would be questionable, and sure to be persistently questioned; whilst a ratification by three-fourths of all the States would be unquestioned and unquestionable."

On Thursday, by the President's direction, a War Department Order was drawn up and issued, putting an end to drafting and recruiting, and the purchase of Military supplies, and removing all restrictions which Military necessity had imposed upon the trade and commerce and intercourse of any one part of the Union with the other. On Friday, the 14th of April, there was a meeting of the Cabinet at noon, to receive a report from General Grant, in person—he having just arrived from the scene of Lee's surrender. Later, the President rode out with Mrs. Lincoln, and talked of the hard time they had had since coming to Washington; "but," continued he, "the War is over, and, with God's blessing, we may hope for four years of Peace and happiness, and then we will go back to Illinois, and pass the rest of our lives in quiet." At Ford's Theatre, that evening, was played "The American Cousin," and it had been announced that both the President and General Grant would be present. Grant, however, was prevented from attending. President Lincoln attended with reluctance—possibly because of a presentiment which he had that day had, that "something serious is going to happen," of which he made mention at the Cabinet meeting aforesaid.

It was about 9 o-clock P.M., that the President, with Mrs. Lincoln, Major Rathbone, and Miss Harris, entered the Theatre, and, after acknowledging with a bow the patriotic acclamations with which the audience saluted him, entered the door of the private box, reserved for his party, which was draped with the folds of the American flag. At half past 10 o'clock, while all were absorbed in the play, a pistol-shot was heard, and a man, brandishing a bloody dagger, was seen to leap to the stage from the President's box, crying "Sic Semper Tyrannis!" His spurred boot, catching in the bunting, tripped him, so that he half fell and injured one leg, but instantly recovered himself, and, shouting "The South is avenged!" rushed across the stage, and disappeared. It was an actor, John Wilkes Booth by name, who—inspired with all the mad, unreasoning, malignant hatred of everything representing Freedom and Union, which was purposely instilled into the minds and hearts of their followers and sympathizers by the Rebel leaders and their chief accomplices in the North—had basely skulked into the box, behind Mr. Lincoln, mortally wounded him with a pistol-bullet, and escaped—after stabbing Major Rathbone for vainly striving to arrest the vile assassin's flight.

Thus this great and good Ruler of our reunited People was foully stricken down in the very moment of his triumph; when the Union troops were everywhere victorious; when Lee had surrendered the chief Army of the downfallen Confederacy; when Johnston was on the point of surrendering the only remaining Rebel force which could be termed an Army; on the self-same day too, which saw the identical flag of the Union, that four years before had been sadly hauled down from the flagstaff of Fort Sumter, triumphantly raised again over that historic fort; when, the War being at an end, everything in the future looked hopeful; at the very time when his merciful and kindly mind was doubtless far away from the mimic scenes upon which he looked, revolving beneficent plans for reconstructing and rebuilding the waste and desolate places in the South which War had made; at this time, of all times, when his clear and just perceptions and firm patriotism were most needed,

[For his last public words, two nights before, had been: "In the present 'situation,' as the phrase goes, it may be my duty to make some new announcement to the people of the South. I am CONSIDERING, and shall not fail to act when satisfied that action will be proper."]

alike by conquerors and conquered, to guide and aid the Nation in the difficult task of reconstruction, and of the new departure, looming up before it, with newer and broader and better political issues upon which all Patriot might safely divide, while all the old issues of States-rights, Secession, Free-Trade, and Slavery, and all the mental and moral leprosy growing out of them, should lie buried far out of sight as dead-and-gone relics of the cruel and devastating War which they alone had brought on! Abraham Lincoln never spoke again. The early beams of the tomorrow's sun touched, but failed to warm, the lifeless remain of the great War-President and Liberator, as they were borne, in mournful silence, back to the White House, mute and ghastly witness of the sheer desperation of those who, although armed Rebellion, in the open field, by the fair and legitimate modes of Military warfare, had ceased, were determined still to keep up that cowardly "fire in the rear" which had been promised to the Rebel leaders by their Northern henchmen and sympathizers.

The assassination of President Lincoln was but a part of the plot of Booth and his murderous Rebel-sympathizing fellow conspirators. It was their purpose also to kill Grant, and Seward, and other prominent members of the Cabinet, simultaneously, in the wild hope that anarchy might follow, and Treason find its opportunity. In this they almost miraculously failed, although Seward was badly wounded by one of the assassins.

That the Rebel authorities were cognizant of, and encouraged, this dastardly plot, cannot be distinctly proven. But, while they naturally would be likely, especially in the face of the storm of public exasperation which it raised throughout the Union, to disavow all knowledge of, or complicity in, the vengeful murder of President Lincoln, and to destroy all evidences possible of any such guilty knowledge or complicity, yet there will ever be a strong suspicion that they were not innocent. From the time when it was first known that Mr. Lincoln had been elected President, the air was full of threats that he should not live to be inaugurated.

That the assassination, consummated in April, 1865, would have taken place in February of 1861, had it not been for the timely efforts of Lieutenant-General Scott, Brigadier-General Stone, Hon. William H. Seward, Frederick W. Seward, Esq., and David S. Bookstaver of the Metropolitan Police of New York—is abundantly shown by Superintendent John A. Kennedy, in a letter of August 13, 1866, to be found in vol. ii., of Lossing's "Civil War in America," pages 147-149, containing also an extract from a letter of General Stone, in which the latter—after mentioning that General Scott and himself considered it "almost a certainty that Mr. Lincoln could not pass Baltimore alive by the train on the day fixed"—proceeds to say: "I recommended that Mr. Lincoln should be officially warned; and suggested that it would be altogether best that he should take the train of that evening from Philadelphia, and so reach Washington early the next day." * * * General Scott, after asking me how the details could be arranged in so short a time, and receiving my suggestion that Mr. Lincoln should be advised quietly to take the evening train, and that it would do him no harm to have the telegraph wires cut for a few hours, he directed me to seek Mr. W. H. Seward, to whom he wrote a few lines, which he handed to me. It was already ten o'clock, and when I reached Mr. Seward's house he had left; I followed him to the Capitol, but did not succeed in finding him until after 12 M. I handed him the General's note; he listened attentively to what I said, and asked me to write down my information and suggestions, and then, taking the paper I had written, he hastily left. The note I wrote was what Mr. Frederick Seward carried to Mr. Lincoln in Philadelphia. Mr. Lincoln has stated that it was this note which induced him to change his journey as he did. The stories of disguise are all nonsense; Mr. Lincoln merely took the sleeping-car in the night train.

Equally certain also, is it, that the Rebel authorities were utterly indifferent to the means that might be availed of to secure success to Rebellion. Riots and arson, were among the mildest methods proposed to be used in the Northern cities, to make the War for the Union a "failure"—as their

Northern Democratic allies termed it—while, among other more devilish projects, was that of introducing cholera and yellow fever into the North, by importing infected rags! Another much-talked-of scheme throughout the War, was that of kidnapping President Lincoln, and other high officials of the Union Government. There is also evidence, that the Rebel chiefs not only received, but considered, the plans of desperadoes and cut-throats looking to the success of the Rebellion by means of assassination. Thus, in a footnote to page 448, vol. ii., of his "Civil War in America," Lossing does not hesitate to characterize Jefferson Davis as "the crafty and malignant Chief Conspirator, who seems to have been ready at all times to entertain propositions to assassinate, by the hand of secret murder, the officers of the Government at Washington;" and, after fortifying that statement by a reference to page 523 of the first volume of his work, proceeds to say: "About the time (July, 1862) we are now considering, a Georgian, named Burnham, wrote to Jefferson Davis, proposing to organize a corps of five hundred assassins, to be distributed over the North, and sworn to murder President Lincoln, members of his Cabinet, and leading Republican Senators, and other supporters of the Government. This proposition was made in writing, and was regularly filed in the 'Confederate War Department,' indorsed 'Respectfully referred to the Secretary of War, by order of the President,' and signed 'J. C Ives.' Other communications of similar tenor, 'respectfully referred' by Jefferson Davis, were placed on file in that 'War Department.'" All the denials, therefore, of the Rebel chieftains, as to their complicity in the various attempts to assassinate Abraham Lincoln, ending with his dastardly murder in April, 1865, will not clear their skirts of the odium of that unparalleled infamy. It will cling to them, living or dead, until that great Day of Judgment when the exact truth shall be made known, and "their sin shall find them out."

[The New York Tribune, August 16, 1885, under the heading "A NARROW ESCAPE OF LINCOLN," quotes an interesting "Omaha Letter, to the St. Paul Pioneer Press," as follows:

"That more than one attempt was made to assassinate Abraham Lincoln is a fact known to John W. Nichols, ex-president of the Omaha Fire Department. Mr. Nichols was one of the body-guard of President Lincoln from the Summer of 1862 until 1865. The following narrative, related to your correspondent by Mr. Nichols, is strictly true, and the incident is not generally known:

One night about the middle of August, 1864, I was doing sentinel duty at the large gate through which entrance was had to the grounds of the Soldiers' Home. The grounds are situated about a quarter of a mile off the Bladensburg road, and are reached by devious driveways. About 11 o'clock I heard a rifle shot in the direction of the city, and shortly afterwards I heard approaching hoof-beats. In two or three minutes a horse came

dashing-up, and I recognized the belated President. The horse was very spirited, and belonged to Mr. Lamon, marshal of the District of Columbia. This horse was Mr. Lincoln's favorite, and when he was in the White House stables he always chose him. As horse and rider approached the gate, I noticed that the President was bareheaded. After assisting him in checking his steed, the President said to me: 'He came pretty near getting away with me, didn't he? He got the bit in his teeth before I could draw the rein.' I then asked him where his hat was, and he replied that somebody had fired a gun off down at the foot of the hill, and that his horse had become scared and jerked his hat off. I led the animal to the Executive Cottage, and the President dismounted and entered. Thinking the affair rather strange, a corporal and myself started in the direction of the place from where the sound of the rifle report had proceeded, to investigate the occurrence. When we reached the spot where the driveway intersects with the main road we found the President's hat—a plain silk hat—and upon examining it we discovered a bullet hole through the crown. The shot had been fired upwards, and it was evident that the person who fired the shot had secreted himself close to the roadside. We listened and searched the locality thoroughly, but to no avail. The next day I gave Mr. Lincoln his hat and called his attention to the bullet hole. He rather unconcernedly remarked that it was put there by some foolish gunner, and was not intended for him. He said, however, that he wanted the matter kept quiet, and admonished us to say nothing about it. We all felt confident that it was an attempt to kill him, and a well-nigh successful one, too. The affair was kept quiet, in accordance with his request. After that, the President never rode alone."]
That this dark and wicked and bloody Rebellion, waged by the upholders and advocates of Slavery, Free Trade, and Secession, had descended so low as to culminate in murder—deliberate, cold-blooded, cowardly murder—at a time when the Southern Conspirators would apparently be the least benefitted by it, was regarded at first as evidencing their mad fatuity; and the public mind was dreadfully incensed.
The successor of the murdered President—Andrew Johnson—lost little time in offering (May the 2d) rewards, ranging from $25,000 to $100,000, for the arrest of Jefferson Davis, Jacob Thompson,
[The same individual at whose death, in 1885, the Secretary of the Interior, ordered the National flag of the Union—which he had swindled, betrayed, fought, spit upon, and conspired against—to be lowered at halfmast over the Interior Departmental Building, at Washington, D. C.]
Clement C. Clay, Beverly Tucker, George N. Sanders, and W. C. Cleary, in a Proclamation which directly charged that they, "and other Rebels and Traitors against the Government of the United States, harbored in Canada," had "incited, concerted, and procured" the perpetration of the appalling crime.

On the 10th of May, one of them, Jacob Thompson, from his place of security, in Canada, published a letter claiming to be innocent; characterized himself as "a persecuted man;" arrayed certain suspicious facts in support of an intimation that Johnson himself was the only one man in the Republic who would be benefited by President Lincoln's death; and, as he was found "asleep" at the "unusual hour" of nine o'clock P.M., of the 14th of April, and had made haste to take the oath of office as President of the United States as soon as the breath had left the body of his predecessor, insinuated that he (Johnson) might with more reason be suspected of "complicity" in "the foul work" than the "Rebels and Traitors" charged with it, in his Proclamation; so charged, for the very purpose—Thompson insinuated— of shielding himself from discovery, and conviction!

But while, for a moment, perhaps, there flitted across the public mind a half suspicion of the possibility of what this Rebel intimated as true, yet another moment saw it dissipated. For the People remembered that between "Andrew Johnson," one of the "poor white trash" of Tennessee, and the "aristocratic Slave-owners" of the South, who headed the Rebellion, there could be neither sympathy nor cooperation—nothing, but hatred; and that this same Andrew Johnson, who, by power of an indomitable will, self-education, and natural ability, had, despite the efforts of that "aristocracy," forced himself upward, step by step, from the tailor's bench, to the successful honors of alderman and Mayor, and then still upward through both branches of his State Legislature, into the House of Representatives and the Senate of the United States—and, in the latter Body, had so gallantly met, and worsted in debate, the chosen representatives of that class upon whose treasonable heads he poured forth in invective, the gathered hatred of a life-time—would probably be the very last man whom these same "aristocratic" Conspirators, "Rebels, and Traitors," would prefer as arbiter of their fate.

The popular feeling responded heartily, at this time, to the denunciations which, in his righteous indignation, he had, in the Senate, and since, heaped upon Rebellion, and especially his declaration that "Treason must be made odious!"—utterances now substantially reiterated by him more vehemently than ever, and multiplied in posters and transparencies and newspapers all over the Land. Thus the public mind rapidly grew to believe it impossible that the Rebel leaders could gain, by the substitution, in the Executive chair, of this harsh, determined, despotic nature, for the mild, kindly, merciful, even-tempered, Abraham Lincoln. With Andrew Johnson for President, the People felt that justice would fall upon the heads of the guilty, and that the Country was safe. And so it happened that, while the mere instruments of the assassination conspiracy were hurried to an ignominious death, in the lull that followed, Jefferson Davis and others of the Rebel chiefs, who had been captured and imprisoned, were allowed to go "Scott-free, without even the semblance of a trial for their Treason!"

It is not the purpose of this work to deal with the history of the Reconstruction or rehabilitation of the Rebel States; to look too closely into the devious ways and subtle methods through and by which the Rebel leaders succeeded in flattering the vanity, and worming themselves into the confidence and control, of Andrew Johnson—by pretending to believe that his occupation of the Presidential Office had now, at last, brought him to their "aristocratic" altitude, and to a hearty recognition by them of his "social equality;" or to follow, either in or out of Congress, the great political conflict, between their unsuspecting Presidential dupe and the Congress, which led to the impeachment trial of President Andrew Johnson, for high crimes and misdemeanors in office, his narrow escape from conviction and deposition, and to much consequent excitement and turmoil among the People, which, but for wise counsels and prudent forethought of the Republican leaders, in both Civil and Military life, might have eventuated in the outbreak of serious civil commotions. Suffice it to say, that in due time; long after the Thirteenth Amendment to the United States Constitution had been ratified by three-fourths of all the States; after Johnson had vexed the White House, with his noisy presence, for the nearly four years succeeding the death of the great and good Lincoln; and after the People, with almost unexampled unanimity, had called their great Military hero, Grant, to the helm of State; the difficult and perplexing problems involved in the Reconstruction of the Union were, at last, successfully solved by the Republican Party, and every State that had been in armed Rebellion against that Union, was not only back again, with a Loyal State Constitution, but was represented in both branches of Congress, and in other Departments of the National Government.

TURNING BACK THE HANDS

And now, the War having ended in the defeat, conquest, and capture, of those who, inspired by the false teachings of Southern leaders, had arrayed themselves in arms beneath the standard of Rebellion, and fought for Sectional Independence against National Union, for Slavery against Freedom, and for Free Trade against a benignant Tariff protective alike to manufacturer, mechanic, and laborer, it might naturally be supposed that, with the collapse of this Rebellion, all the issues which made up "the Cause"—the "Lost Cause," as those leaders well termed it—would be lost with it, and disappear from political sight; that we would never again hear of a Section of the Nation, and last of all the Southern Section, organized, banded together, solidified in the line of its own Sectional ideas as against the National ideas prevailing elsewhere through the Union; that Free Trade, conscious of the ruin and desolation which it had often wrought, and of the awful sacrifices, in blood and treasure, that had been made in its behalf by the conquered South, would slink from sight and hide its famine-breeding front forever; and that Slavery, in all its various disguises, was banished, never more to obtrude its hateful form upon our Liberty-loving Land. That was indeed the supposition and belief which everywhere pervaded the Nation, when Rebellion was conquered by the legions of the Union—and which especially pervaded the South. Never were Rebels more thoroughly exhausted and sick of Rebellion and of everything that led to it, than these. As Badeau said, they made haste "to yield everything they had fought for," and "dreamed not of political power." They had been brought to their knees, suing for forgiveness, and thankful that their forfeit lives were spared.

For awhile, with chastened spirit, the reconstructed South seemed to reconcile itself in good faith to the legitimate results of the War, and all went well. But Time and Peace soon obliterate the lessons and the memories of War. And it was not very long after the Rebellion had ceased, and the old issues upon which it was fought had disappeared from the arena of National politics, when its old leaders and their successors began slowly, carefully, and systematically, to relay the tumbled-down, ruined foundations and walls of the Lost Cause—a work in which, unfortunately, they were too well aided by the mistaken clemency and magnanimity of the Republican Party, in hastily removing the political disabilities of those leaders.

Before proceeding farther, it is necessary to remark here, that, after the suppression of the Rebellion and adoption of the Thirteenth Amendment to the Constitution of the United States, which prohibits Slavery and Involuntary Servitude within the United States, it soon became apparent that it was necessary to the protection of the Freedmen, in the civil and political rights and privileges which it was considered desirable to secure to them, as well as to the creation and fostering of a wholesome loyal sentiment in, and real reconstruction of, the States then lately insurgent, and for certain other reasons, that other safeguards, in the shape of further Amendments to the Constitution, should be adopted.

Accordingly the Fourteenth and Fifteenth Amendments were, on the 16th of June, 1866, and 27th of February, 1869, respectively, proposed by Congress to the Legislatures of the several States, and were declared duly ratified, and a part of the Constitution, respectively on the 28th of July, 1868, and March 30, 1870. Those Amendments were in these words:

"ARTICLE XIV.

"SECTION 1.—All persons born or naturalized in the United States, and subject to the jurisdiction thereof, are citizens of the United States and of the State wherein they reside. No State shall make or enforce any law which shall abridge the privileges or immunities of citizens of the United States; nor shall any State deprive any person of life, liberty, or property, without due process of law; nor deny to any person within its jurisdiction the equal protection of the laws.

"SECTION 2.—Representatives shall be apportioned among the several States according to their respective numbers, counting the whole number of persons in each State, excluding Indians not taxed. But when the right to vote at any election for the choice of electors for President and Vice President of the United States, Representatives in Congress, the Executive and Judicial officers of a State, or the members of the Legislature thereof, is denied to any of the male inhabitants of such State, being twenty-one years of age, and citizens of the United States, or in any way abridged, except for participation in Rebellion, or other crime, the basis of Representation therein shall be reduced in the proportion which the number of such male citizens shall bear to the whole number of male citizens twenty-one years of age in such State.

"SECTION 3.—No person shall be a Senator or Representative in Congress, or Elector of President and Vice-President, or hold any office, civil or military, under the United States, or under any State, who, having previously taken an oath, as a member of Congress, or as an officer of the United States, or as a member of any State Legislature, or as an executive or judicial officer of any State, to support the Constitution of the United States, shall have engaged in Insurrection or Rebellion against the same, or given aid or comfort to the enemies thereof. But Congress may by a vote of two-thirds of each House, remove such disability.

"SECTION 4.—The validity of the public debt of the United States, authorized by law, including debts incurred for payment of pensions and bounties for services in suppressing Insurrection or Rebellion, shall not be questioned. But neither the United States nor any State shall assume or pay any debt or obligation incurred in aid of Insurrection or Rebellion against the United States, or any claim for the loss or Emancipation of any Slave; but all such debts, obligations and claims shall be held illegal and void.

"SECTION 5.—The Congress shall have power to enforce, by appropriate legislation, the provisions of this article."

"ARTICLE XV.

"SECTION 1.—The right of citizens of the United States to vote shall not be denied or abridged by, the United States or by any State on account of race, color, or previous condition of servitude.

"SECTION 2.— The Congress shall have power to enforce this article by appropriate legislation."

It would seem, then, from the provisions of the Thirteenth, Fourteenth, and Fifteenth Amendments to the Constitution, and the Congressional legislation subsequently enacted for the purpose of enforcing them, that not only the absolute personal Freedom of every man, woman, and child in the United States was thus irrevocably decreed; that United States citizenship was clearly defined; that the life, liberty, property, privileges and immunities of all were secured by throwing around them the "equal protection of the laws;" that the right of the United States citizen to vote, was placed beyond denial or abridgment, on "account of race, color, or previous condition of servitude;" but, to make this more certain, the basis of Congressional Representative—apportionment was changed from its former mixed relation, comprehending both persons and "property," so-called, to one of personal numbers—the Black man now counting quite as much as the White man, instead of only three-fifths as much; and it was decreed, that, except for crime, any denial to United States citizens, whether Black or White, of the right to vote at any election of Presidential electors, Congressional Representatives, State Governors, Judges, or Legislative members, "shall" work a reduction, proportioned to the extent of such denial, in the Congressional Representation of the State, or States, guilty of it. As a further safeguard, in the process of reconstruction, none of the insurgent States were rehabilitated in the Union except upon acceptance of those three Amendments as an integral part of the United States Constitution, to be binding upon it; and it was this Constitution as it is, and not the Constitution as it was, that all the Representatives, in both Houses of Congress, from those insurgent States—as well as all their State officers—swore to obey as the supreme law of the Land, when taking their respective oaths of office.

Biding their time, and pretending to act in good faith, as the years rolled by, the distrust and suspicion with which the old Rebel-conspirators had naturally been regarded, gradually lessened in the public mind. With a glad heart, the Congress, year after year, removed the political disabilities from class after class of those who had incurred them, until at last all, so desiring, had been reinstated in the full privileges of citizenship, save the very few unrepentant instigators and leaders of the Rebellion, who, in the depths of that oblivion to which they seemingly had been consigned, continued to nurse the bitterness of their downfall into an implacable hatred of that Republic which had paralyzed the bloody hands of Rebellion, and shattered all their ambitious dreams of Oligarchic rule, if not of Empire.

But, while the chieftains of the great Conspiracy—and of the armed Rebellion itself—remained at their homes unpunished, through the clemency of the American People; the active and malignant minds of some of them were plotting a future triumph for the "Lost Cause," in the overthrow, in consecutive detail, of the Loyal governments of the Southern States, by any and all means which might be by them considered most desirable, judicious, expedient, and effectual; the solidifying of these Southern States into a new Confederation, or league, in fact—with an unwritten but well understood Constitution of its own—to be known under the apparently harmless title of the "Solid South," whose mission it would be to build up, and strengthen, and populate, and enrich itself within the Union, for a time, greater or less, according to circumstances, and in the meanwhile to work up, with untiring devotion and energy, not only to this practical autonomy and Sectional Independence within the Union, but also to a practical re-enslavement of the Blacks, and to the vigorous reassertion and triumph, by the aid of British gold, of those pernicious doctrines of Free-Trade which, while beneficial to the Cotton-lords of the South, would again check and drag down the robust expansion of manufactures and commerce in all other parts of the Land, and destroy the glorious prosperity of farmers, mechanics, and laborers, while at the same time crippling Capital, in the North and West.

In order to accomplish these results—after whatever of suspicion and distrust that might have still remained in Northern minds had been removed by the public declaration in 1874, by one of the ablest and most persuasively eloquent of Southern statesmen, that "The South—prostrate, exhausted, drained of her life-blood as well as of her material resources, yet still honorable and true—accepts the bitter award of the bloody arbitrament without reservation, resolutely determined to abide the result with chivalrous fidelity"—these old Rebel leaders commenced in good earnest to carry out their well organized programme, which they had already experimentally tested, to their own satisfaction, in certain localities.

The plan was this: By the use of shot-guns and rifles, and cavalcades of armed white Democrats, in red shirts, riding around the country at dead of night, whipping prominent Republican Whites and Negroes to death, or shooting or hanging them if thought advisable, such terror would fall upon the colored Republican voters that they would keep away from the polls, and consequently the white Democrats, undeterred by such influences, and on the contrary, eager to take advantage of them, would poll not only a full vote, but a majority vote, on all questions, whether involving the mere election of Democratic officials, or otherwise; and where intimidation of this, or any other kind, should fail, then a resort to be had to whatever devices might be found necessary to make a fraudulent count and return, and thus secure Democratic triumph; and furthermore, when evidences of these intimidations and frauds should be presented to those people of the Union who believe in every citizen of this free Republic having one free vote, and that vote fairly counted, then to laugh the complainants out of Court with the cry that such stories are not true; are "campaign lies" devised solely for political effect; and are merely the product of Republican "outrage mills," ground out, to order.

This plan was first thoroughly tried in Mississippi, and has hence been called the "Mississippi plan." So magically effectual was it, that, with variations adapted to locality and circumstances, this "Mississippi plan" soon enveloped the entire South in its mesh-work of fraud, barbarity, and blood. The massacres, and other outrages, while methodical, were remittent, wave-like, sometimes in one Southern State, sometimes another, and occurring only in years of hot political conflict, until one after another of those States had, by these crimes, been again brought under the absolute control of the old Rebel leaders. By 1876, they had almost succeeded in their entire programme. They had captured all, save three, of the Southern States, and strained every nerve and every resource of unprincipled ingenuity, of bribery and perjury, after the Presidential election of that year had taken place, in the effort to defeat the will of the People and "count in," the Presidential candidate of the Democratic Party.

[The shameful history of the "Tilden barrel" and the "Cipher Dispatches" is too fresh in the public mind to be entirely forgotten,]

Failing in this effort, the very failure became a grievance. On the principle of a fleeing thief diverting pursuit by shouting "Stop thief," the cry of "fraud" was raised by the Democratic leaders, North and South, against the Republican Party, and was iterated and reiterated so long and loudly, that soon they actually began, themselves, to believe, that President Hayes had been "counted in," by improper methods! At all events, under cover of the hue and cry thus raised, the Southern leaders hurried up their work of Southern solidification, by multiplied outrages on the "Mississippi plan," so that, by 1880, they were ready to dictate, and did dictate, the Democratic Presidential nominations.

[Senator Wallace, of Pennsylvania, telegraphed from Cincinnati his congratulations to General Hancock, and added: "General Buell tells me that Murat Halsted says Hancock's nomination by the Confederate Brigadiers sets the old Rebel yell to the music of the Union." In the Convention which nominated Hancock, Wade Hampton made a speech, saying; "On behalf of the 'Solid South,' that South which once was arrayed against the great soldier of Pennsylvania, I stand here to pledge you its solid vote. [cheers] * * * There is no name which is held in higher respect among the people of the South, than that of the man you have given to us as our standard-bearer." And afterward, in a speech at Staunton, Virginia, the same Southern leader, in referring to the action of the Democratic Convention at Cincinnati, said: "There was but one feeling among the Southern delegates. That feeling was expressed when we said to our Northern Democratic brethren 'Give us an available man.' They gave us that man."]

While these old Rebel leaders of the South had insisted upon, and had succeeded in, nominating a man whose record as a Union soldier would make him popular in the North and West, and while their knowledge of his availability for Southern purposes would help them in their work of absolutely solidifying the South, they took very good care also to press forward their pet Free-Trade issue—that principle so dear to the hearts of the Rebel Cotton-lords that, as has already been hinted, they incorporated it into their Constitution of Confederation in these words:

"SEC. 8.—Congress shall have power to lay and collect taxes, duties, imposts and excises for revenue necessary to pay the debts, provide for the common defense, and carry on the Government of the Confederate States; but no bounty shall be granted from the Treasury, nor shall any duty or tax on importation from Foreign Nations be laid to promote or foster any branch of industry."

It may also be remarked that, under the inspiration of those Southern leaders who afterward rebelled, it had been laid down as Democratic doctrine, in the National Democratic platform of 1856—and "reaffirmed" as such, in 1860—that "The time has come for the People of the United States to declare themselves in favor of * * * progressive Free-Trade. * * * That justice and sound policy forbid the Federal Government to foster one branch of industry to the detriment of another." But, by 1864, the Republican Protective-Tariff of 1860, had so abundantly demonstrated, to all our people engaged in industrial occupations, the beneficence of the great principle of home industrial Protection, that Tariff-agitation actually ceased, and the National Democratic platform of that year had nothing to say in behalf of Free-Trade!

After the close of the War, however, at the very first National Democratic Convention, in 1868, at which there were delegations from the lately rebellious States, the question was at once brought to the front, and, under the inspiration of the old Rebel leaders aforesaid, the Democratic platform again raised the banner of Free-Trade by declaring for a Tariff for revenue. But the mass of the People, at that time still freshly remembered the terrible commercial disasters and industrial depressions which had befallen the Land, through the practical operation of that baleful Democratic Free-Trade doctrine, before the Rebellion broke out, and sharply contrasted the misery and poverty and despair of those dark days of ruin and desolation, with the comfort and prosperity and hopefulness which had since come to them through the Republican Protective-Tariff Accordingly, the Republican Presidential candidate, representing the great principle of Protection to American Industries, was elected over the Democratic Free-Trade candidate, by 214 to 71 electoral votes-or nearly three to one!

Taught, by this lesson, that the People were not yet sufficiently prepared for a successful appeal in behalf of anything like Free-Trade, the next National Democratic Convention, (that of 1872), under the same Southern inspiration, more cautiously declared, in its platform, that "Recognizing that there are in our midst, honest but irreconcilable differences of opinion, with regard to the respective systems of Protection and Free-Trade, we remit the discussion of the subject to the People in their Congressional districts, and to the decision of the Congress thereon, wholly free from Executive interference or dictation." The People, however, rebuked the moral cowardice thus exhibited by the Democracy—in avoiding a direct issue on the doctrine which Democracy itself had galvanized at least into simulated life,—by giving 286 electoral votes to the Republican candidate, to 63 for the Democratic,—or in the proportion of nearly five to one.

Warned, by this overwhelming defeat, not to flinch from, or avoid, or try to convert the great National question of Tariff, into a merely local one, the National Democratic platform of 1876, at the instigation of the old Rebel leaders of the now fast solidifying South, came out flat-footedly again with the "demand that all Custom-house taxation shall be only for revenue." This time, the electoral vote stood almost evenly divided, viz.: for the Republican candidate, 185; for the Democratic candidate, 184;—a result so extremely close, as to lead to the attempted perpetration of great frauds against the successful candidate; the necessary settlement of the questions growing out of them, by an Electoral commission—created by Congress at the instance of the Democratic Party; great irritation, among the defeated Democracy, over the just findings of that august Tribunal; and to the birth of the alleged Democratic "grievance," aforesaid.

The closeness of this vote—their almost triumph, in 1876,—encouraged the Solid South to press upon the National Democratic Convention of 1880, the expediency of adopting a Free-Trade "plank" similar to that with which, in 1876, they had so nearly succeeded. Hence the Democratic platform of 1880, also declared decidedly for "A Tariff for revenue only."

The old Rebel leaders, at last in full control of the entire Democratic Party, had now got things pretty much as they wanted them. They had created that close corporation within the Union—that imperium in imperio that oligarchically—governed league of States (within the Republic of the United States) which they termed the "Solid South," and which would vote as a unit, on all questions, as they directed; they had dictated the nomination, by the Democratic Party, of a Presidential candidate who would not dare to act counter to their wishes; and their pet doctrine of Free-Trade was held up, to the whole Democratic front, under the attractive disguise of a Tariff for revenue only.

[As Ex-Senator Toombs, of Georgia, wrote: "The old boys of the South will see that 'Hancock' does the fair thing by them. In other words, he will run the machine to suit them, or they will run the thing themselves. They are not going to be played with any longer."]

In other words, they had already secured a "Solid South," an "available" candidate, and an "expedient" Free-Trade platform. All that remained for them, at this stage, to do, was to elect the candidate, and enact their Free-Trade doctrine into legislation. This was their current work, so to speak—to be first attended to—but not all their work; for one of the most brilliant and candid of their coadjutors had said, only a few months before: "We do not intend to stop until we have stricken the last vestige of your War measures from the Statute-book."

Unfortunately, however, for their plans, an attempt made by them, under the lead of Mr. Morrison of Illinois, in 1876, to meddle with the Republican Protective-Tariff, had caused considerable public alarm, and had been credited with having much to do with a succeeding monetary panic, and industrial depression. Another and more determined effort, made by them in 1878, under the lead of their old Copperhead ally, Fernando Wood, to cut down the wise Protective duties imposed by the Tariff Act, about 15 per cent.,—together with the cold-blooded Free-Trade declaration of Mr. Wood, touching his ruinous Bill, that "Its reductions are trifling as compared with what they should be. * * * If I had the power to commence de novo, I should reduce the duties 50 per cent., instead of less than 15 per cent., upon an average as now proposed,"—an effort which was narrowly, and with great difficulty, defeated by the Republicans, aided by a mere handful of others,—had also occasioned great excitement throughout the Country, the suspension and failure of thousands of business firms, the destruction of confidence in the stability and profitableness of American industries, and great consequent suffering, and enforced idleness, to the working men and working women of the Land.

The sad recollection of these facts—made more poignant by the airy declaration of the Democratic Presidential candidate, that the great National question of the Tariff is a mere "local issue,"—was largely instrumental, in connection with the insolent aggressiveness of the Southern leaders, in Congress, in occasioning their defeat in the Presidential contest of 1880, the Republican candidate receiving 214 electoral votes, while the Democratic candidate received but 155 electoral votes.

In 1882, the House of Representatives was under Republican control, and, despite determined Democratic resistance, created a Tariff-commission, whose duty it was "to take into consideration, and to thoroughly investigate, all the various questions relating to the agricultural, commercial, mercantile, manufacturing, mining, and (other) industrial interests of the United States, so far as the same may be necessary to the establishment of a judicious Tariff, or a revision of the existing Tariff, upon a scale of justice to all interests."

That same year, in the face of most protracted and persistent opposition by the great bulk of Democratic members, both of the Senate and House of Representatives, and an effort to substitute for it the utterly ruinous Democratic Free-Trade Tariff of 1846, the Bill recommended by this Republican Tariff-commission, was enacted; and, in 1883, a modified Tariff-measure, comprehending a large annual reduction of import duties, while also carefully preserving the great Republican American principle of Protection, was placed by the Republicans on the Statute-book, despite the renewed and bitter opposition of the Democrats, who, as usual, fought it desperately in both branches of Congress. But Republican efforts failed in 1884, in the interest of the wool-growers of the country, to restore the Protective-duties on wool, which had been sacrificed, in 1883, to an exigency created by Democratic opposition to them.

Another Democratic effort, in the direction of Free-Trade, known as "the Morrison Tariff-Bill of 1884," was made in the latter year, which, besides increasing the free-list, by adding to it salt, coal, timber, and wood unmanufactured, as well as many manufactures thereof, decreased the import duties "horizontally" on everything else to the extent of twenty per cent. The Republicans, aided by a few Democrats, killed this undigested and indigestible Democratic Bill, by striking out its enacting clause.

By this time, however, by dint of the incessant special-pleading in behalf of the obnoxious and un-American doctrine of Free-Trade,—or the nearest possible approach to it, consistent with the absolutely essential collection of revenues for the mere support of the Government —indulged in (by some of the professors) in our colleges of learning; through a portion of the press; upon the stump; and in Congress; together with the liberal use of British gold in the wide distribution of printed British arguments in its favor,—this pernicious but favorite idea of the Solid South had taken such firm root in the minds of the greater part of the Democratic Party in the North and West, as well as the South, that a declaration in the National Democratic platform in its favor was now looked for, as a matter of course. The "little leaven" of this monstrous un-American heresy seemed likely to leaven "the whole mass" of the Democracy.

But, as in spite of the tremendous advantage given to that Party by the united vote of the Solid South, the Presidential contest of 1884 was likely to be so close that, to give Democracy any chance to win, the few Democrats opposed to Free-Trade must be quieted, the utterances of the Democratic National Platform of that year, on the subject, were so wonderfully pieced, and ludicrously intermixed, that they could be construed to mean "all things to all men."

At last, after an exciting campaign, the Presidential election of 1884 was held, and for the first time since 1856, the old Free-Trade Democracy of the South could rejoice over the triumph of their Presidential candidate.

Great was the joy of the Solid South! At last, its numberless crimes against personal Freedom, and political Liberty, would reap a generous harvest. At last, participation in Rebellion would no more be regarded as a blot upon the political escutcheon. At last, commensurate rewards for all the long years of disconsolate waiting, and of hard work in night ridings, and house-burnings, and "nigger"-whippings, and "nigger"-shootings, and "nigger"-hangings, and ballot-box stuffings, and all the other dreadful doings to which these old leaders were impelled by a sense of Solid-Southern patriotism, and pride of race, and lust for power, would come, and come in profusion.

Grand places in the Cabinet, and foreign Missions, for the old Rebels of distinction, now Chiefs of the "Solid-Southern" Conspiracy, and for those other able Northern Democrats who had helped them, during or since the Rebellion; fat consulates abroad, for others of less degree; post-offices, without stint, for the lesser lights; all this, and more, must now come. The long-hidden light of a glorious day was about to break. The "restoration of the Government to the principles and practices of the earlier period," predicted by the unreconstructed "Rebel chieftains" those "same principles for which they fought for four years" the principles of Southern Independence, Slavery, Free Trade and Oligarchic rule—were now plainly in sight, and within reach!

The triumph of the Free-Trade Democracy, if continued to another

Presidential election, would make Free-Trade a certainty. The old forms of Slavery, to be sure, were dead beyond reanimation—perhaps; but, in their place, were other forms of Slavery, which attracted less attention and reprobation from the World at large, and yet were quite as effectual for all Southern purposes. The system of Peonage and contracted convict-labor, growing out of the codes of Black laws, were all-sufficient to keep the bulk of the Negro race in practical subjection and bondage. The solidifying of the South had already made the South not only practically independent within the Union, but the overshadowing power, potential enough to make, and unmake, the rulers and policies of the Democratic Party, and of that Union.

This, indeed, was a grand outcome for the tireless efforts of the once defeated Conspirators! And as to Oligarchal rule—the rule of the few (and those the Southern chiefs) over the many,—was not that already accomplished? For these old Rebel leaders and oligarchs who had secured the supreme rule over the Solid South, had also, through their ability to wield the power of that Solid South within the Union, actually secured the power of practically governing the entire Union!

That Union, then, which we have been wont to look upon as the grandest, noblest, freest, greatest Republic upon Earth,—is it really such, in all respects, at the present? Does the Free Republic of the United States exist, in fact, to-day?

WHAT NEXT

And what next? Aye, what next? Do the patriotic, innocent-minded lovers of a Republican form of Government imagine, for an instant, that all danger to its continued existence and well-being has ceased to threaten?—that all the crises perilous to that beneficent popular governmental form have vanished?—that the climacteric came, and went, with the breaking out, and suppression, of the Rebellion?—and that there is nothing alarming in the outlook? Quite likely. The public mind has not yet been aroused to a sense of the actual revolution against Republican form of government that has already taken place in many of the Southern States, much less as to the likelihood of things to come. The people of any one of the Western, or Northern States,—take New York, for example,—feel prosperous and happy under the beneficent workings of the Republican Protective-Tariff system. Business, of all sorts, recovering from the numerous attacks made upon that prime bulwark of our American industries, if only let alone, will fairly hum, and look bright, so far as "the Almighty dollar" is concerned. They know they have their primaries and conventions, in their wards and counties throughout their State, and their State Conventions, and their elections. They know that the voice of the majority of their own people, uttered through the sacred ballot-box, is practically the Vox Dei—and that all bow to it. They know also, that this State government of theirs, with all its ramifications—whether as to its Executive, its Legislative, its Judicial, and other officials, either elective or appointed—is a Republican form of government, in the American sense—in the sense contemplated by the Fathers, when they incorporated into the revered Constitution of our Country the vital words: "The United States shall guarantee to every State in this Union a Republican Form of government." But they do not realize the vastly different condition of things in many States of the Solid South, nor how it affects themselves.

And what is this "republican" form of government, thus pledged? It is true that there are not wanting respectable authorities whose definitions of the words "republic," and "republican," are strongly inharmonious with their true meaning, as correctly understood by the great bulk of Americans. Thus, Brande asserts that "A republic may be either a democracy or an aristocracy!"—and proceeds to say: "In the former, the supreme power is vested in the whole body of the people, or in representatives elected by the people; in the latter, it is vested in a nobility, or a privileged class of comparatively a small number of persons." John Adams also wrote: "The customary meanings of the words republic and commonwealth have been infinite. They have been applied to every Government under heaven; that of Turkey and that of Spain, as well as that of Athens and of Rome, of Geneva and San Marino." But the true meaning of the word "republican" as applied to a "form of government," and as commonly and almost invariably understood by those who, above all others in the wide World, should best understand and appreciate its blessings—to wit: the American People has none of the looseness and indefiniteness which these authorities throw about it.

The prevailing and correct American idea is that "Republican" means: of, or pertaining to, a Republic; that "Republic" means a thing, affair, or matter, closely related to, and touching the "public;" and that the "public" are the "people"—not a small proportion of them, but "the people at large," the whole community, the Nation, the commonalty, the generality. Hence, "a Republican form of government" is, in their opinion, plainly that form which is most closely identified with, and representative of, the generality or majority of the people; or, in the language of Dr. J. E. Worcester, it is "That form of government or of a State, in which the supreme power is vested in the people, or in representatives elected by the people."

It is obvious that there can be no such thing as "a republic," which is, at the same time, "an aristocracy;" for the moment that which was "a republic" becomes "an aristocracy," that moment it ceases to be "a republic." So also can there be no such thing as "a republic" which is "an oligarchy," for, as "a republic" is a government of the many, or, as President Lincoln well termed it, "a government of the people, by the people, for the people"—so it must cease to be "a republic," when the supreme power is in the hands of the oligarchic few.

There can be but two kinds of republics proper—one a democratic republic, which is impossible for a great and populous Nation like ours, but which may have answered for some of the small republics of ancient Greece; the other, a representative republic, such as is boasted by the United States. And this is the kind palpably meant by the Fathers, when, for the very purpose of nipping in the bud any anti-republican Conspiracy likely to germinate from Slavery, they inserted in the Great Charter of American Liberties the solemn and irrevocable mandate: "The United States shall guarantee to every State in this Union a Republican Form of Government." That they meant this majority rule—this government by the many, instead of the few—this rule of the People, as against any possible minority rule, by, or through, oligarchs or aristocrats, is susceptible of proof in other ways.

It is a safe guide, in attempting to correctly expound the Constitution of the United States, to be careful that the construction insisted on, is compatible and harmonious with the spirit of that great instrument; so that—as was said by an eloquent and distinguished Massachusetts statesman of twenty years ago, in discussing this very point—"the guarantee of a Republican form of government must have a meaning congenial with the purposes of the Constitution." Those purposes, of course, are expressed in its preamble, or in the body of the instrument, or in both. The preamble itself, in this case, is sufficient to show them. It commences with the significant words: "We THE PEOPLE of the United States"—words, instinct with the very consciousness of the possession of that supreme power by the People or public, which made this not only a Nation, but a Republic; and, after stating the purposes or objects sought by the People in thus instituting this Republic, proceeds to use that supreme political power vested in them, by ordaining and establishing "this CONSTITUTION for the United States of America." And, from the very first article, down to the last, of that "Constitution," or "structure," or "frame," or "form" of government, already self-evidently and self-consciously and avowedly Republican, that form is fashioned into a distinctively representative Republican government.

The purposes themselves, as declared in the preamble, for which the People of the United States thus spake this representative Republic into being, are also full of light. Those purposes were "to form a more perfect Union, establish Justice, insure domestic Tranquillity, provide for the common defense, promote the General Welfare, and secure the Blessings of Liberty to ourselves and our Posterity."

How is it possible, for instance, that "the Blessings of Liberty" are to be secured to "ourselves and our Posterity," if citizens of the United States, despite the XVth Amendment of that Constitution, find—through the machinations of political organizations—their right to vote, both abridged and denied, in many of the States, "on account of race, color, or previous condition of servitude?" How, if, in such States, "the right of the people to be secure in their persons, houses, and effects, against unreasonable searches and seizures," is habitually violated, despite the IVth Amendment of that Constitution? How, if, in such States, persons are notoriously and frequently "deprived of life, liberty, or property, without due process of law," in violation of the Vth Amendment of that Constitution? Yet such is the state of affairs generally prevalent in many States of the Solid South.

These provisions in the Constitution were, with others, placed there for the very purpose of securing "the Blessings of Liberty to ourselves and our Posterity," of promoting the "General Welfare," of establishing "Justice," of insuring "domestic Tranquillity" and making "a more perfect Union"—and the violation of those provisions, or any one of them, in any part of our Land, by any part of our People, in any one of the States, is not only subversive of the Constitution, and revolutionary, but constitutes a demand, in itself, upon the National Government, to obey that imperative mandate of the Constitution (Sec. 4, article IV.) comprehended in the words: "The United States SHALL guarantee to every State in this Union a Republican Form of Government."

[The meaning of these words is correctly given in an opinion of Justice Bronson of New York (4 Hill's Reports, 146) in these words:

"The meaning of the section then seems to be, that no member of the State shall be disfranchised or deprived of any of his rights or privileges unless the matter shall be adjudged against him upon trial had according to the course of common law. The words 'due process of law' cannot mean less than a prosecution or suit instituted and conducted according to the prescribed forms and solemnities for ascertaining guilt or determining the title to property."]

It is well that the truth should be spoken out, and known of all men. The blame for this condition of things belongs partly to the Republican Party. The question is sometimes asked: "If these outrages against citizenship, against the purity of the ballot, against humanity, against both the letter and spirit of the Constitution of our Republic, are perpetrated, why is it that the Republican Party—so long in power during their alleged perpetration—did not put a stop to them?" The answer is: that while there are remedial measures, and measures of prevention, fully warranted by the Constitution—while there are Constitutional ways and means for the suppression of such outrages—yet, out of exceeding tenderness of heart, which prompted the hope and belief that the folly of continuing them must ere long come home to the Southern mind and conscience, the Republican Party has been loath to put them in force. The—best remedy of all, and the best manner of administering it, lies with the people themselves, of those States where these outrages are perpetrated. Let them stop it. The People of the United States may be long-suffering, and slow to wrath; but they will not permit such things to continue forever.

When the Rebellion was quelled, the evil spirit which brought it about should have been utterly crushed out, and none of the questions involved in it should have been permitted to be raised again. But the Republican Party acted from its heart, instead of its head. It was merciful, forgiving, and magnanimous. In the magnificent sweep of its generosity to the erring son, it perhaps failed to insure the exact justice to the other sons which was their right. For, as has already been shown in these pages, Free-Trade, imbedded in the Rebel Constitution, as well as Slavery, entered into and became a part, and an essential part, of the Rebellion against the Union—to triumph with Slavery, if the Rebellion succeeded—to fall with Slavery, if the Rebellion failed. And, while Slavery and Free-Trade, were two leading ideas inspiring the Southern Conspirators and leaders in their Rebellion; Freedom to Man, and Protection to Labor, were the nobler ideas inspiring those who fought for the Union.

The Morrill-Tariff of 1860, with modifications to it subsequently made by its Republican friends, secured to the Nation, through the triumph of the Union arms, great and manifold blessings and abundant prosperity flowing from the American Protective policy; while the Emancipation proclamations, together with the Constitutional amendments, and Congressional legislation, through the same triumph, and the acceptance of the legitimate results of the War, gave Freedom to all within the Nation's bound aries. This, at least, was the logical outcome of the failure of the Rebellion. Such was the general understanding, on all sides, at the conclusion of the War. Yet the Republican Party, in failing to stigmatize the heresy of Free Trade—which had so large an agency in bringing about the equally heretical doctrines of State Sovereignty and the right of Secession, and Rebellion itself,—as an issue or question settled by the War, as a part and parcel of the Rebellion, was guilty of a grave fault of omission, some of the ill-effects of which have already been felt, while others are yet to come. For, quickly after the War of the Rebellion closed,—as has been already mentioned—the defeated Rebel leaders, casting in their lot with their Democratic friends and allies, openly and without special rebuke, prevailed upon the National Democracy to adopt the Rebel Free-Trade Shibboleth of "a Tariff for revenue;" and that same Democracy, obtaining power and place, through violence and fraud and falsehood at the so-called "elections" in the Solid Southern States, now threatens the Country once more with iniquitous Free-Trade legislation, and all its attendant train of commercial disasters and general industrial ruin.

Were Abraham Lincoln able bodily to revisit the United States to-day, how his keen gray eyes would open in amazement, to find that many legitimate fruits of our Union victories had been filched from us; that —save the honorable few, who, accepting the legitimate results of the War, were still honestly striving for the success of principles harmonizing with such results, and inuring to the general welfare—they who strove with all their might to wreck the Government,—were now,—through the fraudulent and forcible restriction of voters in their right to vote—at the helm of State; that these, who sought to ruin the Nation, had thus wrongfully usurped its rule; that Free-Trade—after "running-a-muck" of panic and disaster, from the birth of the Republic, to the outbreak of the Rebellion, with whose failure it should naturally have expired—was now reanimated, and stood, defiantly threatening all the great industries of our Land; that all his own painstaking efforts, and those of the band of devoted Patriots who stood by him to free the Southern Slaves, had mainly resulted in hiding from sight the repulsive chains of enforced servitude, under the outward garb of Freedom; that the old Black codes had simply been replaced by enactments adapted to the new conditions; that the old system of African Slavery had merely been succeeded by the heartless and galling system of African Peonage; that the sacrifices made by him—including that of his martyrdom—had, to a certain extent, been made in vain; that all the sacrifices, the sorrows, the sufferings, of this Nation, made in blood, in tears, and in vast expenditures of time and treasure, had, in some degree, and in a certain sense, been useless; that the Union, to be sure, was saved—but saved to be measurably perverted from its grand purpose; that the power which animated Rebellion and which was supposed to have expired in the "last ditch" with the "Lost Cause" had, by political legerdemain and jugglery and violence, been regained; that the time had actually come for Patriots to take back seats, while unrepentant Rebels came to the front; that the Republic still lived, but only by sufferance, with the hands of Southern oligarchs about its palpitating throat—a Republic, not such as he expected, where all men are equal before the law, and protected in their rights, but where the rights of a certain class are persistently trampled under foot; that the people of the Northern, Middle, and Western States, observing nothing beyond their own vicinage, so to speak, and finding that each of their own States is still Republican in its form of government, persistently, and perversely, shut their eyes to the election terrorism practiced in the Solid South by, which the 16 solid, Southern States were, and are, solidified by these conspiring oligarchs into one compact, and powerful, political mass, ever ready to be hurled, in and out of Congress, against the best interests of the Nation—16 States, not all "Republican" in form, but many of them Despotisms, in substance,—16 States, misnamed "Democratic," many of them ruled not by a majority, but by an Oligarch-ridden minority—16 States, leagued, banded, bound solidly together, as one great controlling Oligarchy, to hold, in its merciless and selfish hands, the balance of power within this Republican Union; and that these confederated Southern States are now actually able to dictate to all the other States of the Union, the particular man, or men, to whose rule the Nation must submit, and the particular policy, or policies, which the Nation must adopt and follow:

"What next?"—you ask—"What next?" Alas, it is not difficult to predict! Power, lawlessly gained, is always mercilessly used. Power, usurped, is never tamely surrendered. The old French proverb, that "revolutions never go

backward," is as true to-day, as when it was written. Already we see the signs of great preparations throughout the Solid South. Already we hear the shout of partisan hosts marshalled behind the leaders of the disarmed Rebellion, in order that the same old political organization which brought distress upon this Land shall again control the Government. Already the spirit of the former aggressiveness is defiantly bestirring itself. The old chieftains intend to take no more chances. They feel that their Great Conspiracy is now assured of success, inside the Union. They hesitate not to declare that the power once held by them, and temporarily lost, is regained. Like the Old Man of the Sea, they are now on top, and they:
MEAN TO KEEP THERE—IF THEY CAN.

www.ingramcontent.com/pod-product-compliance
Lightning Source LLC
Chambersburg PA
CBHW070819290526
45795CB00002B/765